Kodak

GUIDE
America's National Parks
By Michael Frome

POPULAR LIBRARY • NEW YORK

AUTHOR'S NOTE

Michael Frome, one of the country's foremost authors on conservation and travel, knows and loves the national parks as few people do. His travels have taken him from Hawaii and Alaska across the country, and to the Virgin Islands, always adding to his firsthand knowledge of the park scenes and of the scientific, historic, and recreational values they hold for all. Park superintendents, rangers, historians, and naturalists are among his close friends and frequent traveling companions.

Mr. Frome's books and magazine articles have guided millions of readers in appreciation of America's natural treasures. His popular work *Strangers in High Places—The Story of the Great Smoky Mountains* received the Thomas Wolfe Memorial Award and is widely praised as the finest profile on any national park. He is also the author of the popular *Rand McNally National Park Guide, The Varmints—Our Unwanted Wildlife, Whose Woods These Are,* and other books.

He is conservation editor of *Field & Stream;* contributing editor of *Changing Times,* the Kiplinger magazine; featured columnist of *American Forests;* and a frequent contributor to major national publications. Mr. Frome is a former president of the Society of American Travel Writers. He lives with his wife and two teen-age children near Alexandria, Virginia.

CONTENTS

FOREWORD

For eight years, while Secretary of the Interior, the national parks were an intimate part of my life.

I had always been a hiker and camper, a deriver of sustenance from fresh air and far vistas. I always will be. And from now on, my personal park safaris will be enhanced by knowledge of the remarkable capabilities of the National Park Service and of the public that holds these areas dear.

Some of the most dynamic meetings held in my office at Interior were with officials of the National Park Service, mapping strategy to enlarge the park system with outstanding new areas like Canyonlands and the North Cascades. I worked often with members of Congress who were themselves devoted park experts, as well as with scientists, scholars, outdoorsmen, friends and critics—all of whom made important contributions to the scope and quality of the National Park System in the 1960's.

In addition, treasured hours were spent on field trips, discovering the parks as all visitors discover them. Some trips were with my family or adventuresome colleagues; some of the most memorable were with Mrs. Lyndon B. Johnson, who as First Lady did so much to encourage natural beauty preservation and assure its ascendancy in our national priorities.

Parks are popular; the number of visitors has outrun all predictions. Thus, I feel, this Kodak Guide comes at an auspicious time and will be a welcome addition to the practical literature on the national parks.

I know the author, Michael Frome, as a skillful guide and a true conservationist. Kodak and he make an ideal team, for both have belief in insight, and both hold high standards of public service.

The reader of this book will find it opens new dimensions of seeing the outdoors and of translating his unique vision into photographic record. Some of the most esteemed authorities on America's national parks are its photographers. The park photographer will find that the suggestions in this book can be applied just as successfully to the stream valleys, the hillsides, and the vistas and vignettes of nature close to his home. Every community needs to see and save those choice spots, so the skilled photographer has a special opportunity to become the conservation expert right in his own region.

Wherever the reader of this book may go, I wish him a rewarding journey—good picture-taking.

STEWART L. UDALL

PICTURE-TAKING AND THE PARKS

The national parks are known and loved by all the people of the United States.

The parks rank among the foremost destinations Americans visit during the course of their vacation travels, for these incomparable areas constitute a gallery of treasures—the U.S.A. at its finest.

But the national parks are more than tourist attractions in the ordinary sense. They are native-life communities, or *ecosystems,* composed of trees, birds, animals, fish, shrubs, flowers, soil, water, and air—all interdependent, dynamic, and ever-changing. The National Park Service today strives to interpret these features so that visitors understand the *total* environment and man's need to respect natural resources.

There is scarcely a better way of perceiving and appreciating the interwoven web of life in a national park than through the eye of a camera.

The wonders of the natural environment can be multiplied with every picture, yet the environment need not be altered in the process. The photo-visitor can "collect" and interpret flowers, rocks, animals, twilights, and night scenes without scarring the land.

Commercial uses are prohibited in the parks, but the visitor with camera can derive education and true inspiration that will last him a lifetime. As the National Park Service aptly states, a camera lets one ". . . take nothing but pictures, leave nothing but footprints."

The 200-plus units of the National Park System preserve many priceless portions of the American tableau. The national monuments and national historic sites chronicle ancient Indian cliff dwellings, missions, battlefields, the homes of Presidents and other citizens of special note. National recreation areas provide for full enjoyment of the outdoors in a pleasing environment, while protecting outstanding features of scenery, history, and wildlife.

The thirty-four national parks are the heart of the system. They span the sweep of nature, ranging from seashore to desert to forest to glacial peaks high above timberline. Yellowstone, the first national park, was established in 1872—the first national park anywhere in the world. It was a revolutionary idea in that age to safeguard unimpaired a natural environment of wilderness life for the benefit of future generations.

The national parks have proved their value many times over as sanctuaries of nature, in which vanishing plant and animal species are granted the right of survival. The parks are sanctuaries of man as well, granting him relief from the tensions of an urbanized civilization and a brief return to the natural world.

Visiting the national parks deserves time, patience, and planning. So does photography. Good pictures *may* come by accident, but you cannot count on many that way. Shooting in your own familiar backyard is one thing. On a trip, you're suddenly in a strange new place. The excellence of your results will depend heavily on thought and planning in advance of picture-taking, even before leaving home. Learn the details about each park you intend to visit. It will be helpful to write to each park headquarters for its informational brochure. (You can also use these later for factual reference when putting a slide or movie show together.) We've listed the address of the park headquarters at the beginning of the section for each park.

The objective of this pre-travel "homework" is to know what you want to shoot *before* you get where you're going. Such familiarity with the parks will also help you to enjoy them better, to deepen your understanding and appreciation more than if you arrive "cold." On the basis of the maps and facts you accumulate, plan a realistic schedule for what you want to see and photograph. You cannot encompass a whole continent, or even the West, in two weeks. Slow down, eliminate chance as best you can, and stick to your schedule. You'll get more out of your trip, and certainly more good pictures, if you do.

As part of pre-trip preparations, check your camera equipment. It would be disappointing to discover that your camera wasn't working during your trip or that you didn't have everything you needed. By all means, shoot a test roll of film and *see the results* before your trip. This is to make sure the camera is working properly and that you know how to work with it. Check your flash batteries, too—you will want to shoot with flash in hotels and museums, where allowed, as well as outdoors on dark days. Take along a spare set of fresh batteries, and keep battery and equipment contacts clean by wiping them with a rough cloth or pencil eraser.

It's unreasonable to expect that the sun will shine every day you're traveling in the parks. Some pictures are going to be taken on overcast or even rainy days, or they won't be taken at all. Do you know how to expose color film under such conditions? Better learn before you leave home. Consult the instruction sheet packed with every roll of Kodak color film; indeed, it's full of information to help you get better pictures. Choose the right film for the results you want, using the accompanying table as a guide. Film comes in different sizes for different cameras, and different types for different kinds of pictures. Your end result, whether black-and-white prints, color prints, or color slides, depends on the type of film you put in the camera. Since dark days require high-speed film for hand-held shots, it may be wise to purchase such special film before reaching the national parks; some concessioners are well stocked to meet most needs, but others carry only the "general-purpose" types of film.

Besides your flash unit, other items of equipment will prove helpful in the parks. A wide-angle lens captures the scope of mountain vistas. A telephoto lens helps bring distant formations close up and is especially useful in photographing animals and birds. If you do not have elaborate close-up attachments, simple, inexpensive close-up lenses that fit over your camera's lens are useful. A modern tripod, lightweight and condensable into pocket-size packages, may also be a handy item to hold the camera steady for long exposures. You may also want to take along KODAK Prepaid Processing Mailers, which you can get at your dealer's. Anywhere along the way you can put the exposed Kodak color film into the mailer, attach postage stamps, and mail it to the nearest Kodak processing laboratory. The pictures will be waiting for you when you return home. Or, you can have them mailed to a friend who will advise you on how you're doing.

KODAK Color Films (and Abbreviations)	Use For	ASA Speed	Light Source	Sizes Available
KODACHROME II, Daylight Type (K)	Color Slides	25	Daylight or Blue Flash	135-20, 135-36, 828
KODACHROME-X (KX)	Color Slides	64	Daylight or Blue Flash	135-20, 135-36, 126-20
EKTACHROME-X (EX)	Color Slides	64	Daylight or Blue Flash	135-20, 135-36, 126-20, 828, 127, 620, 120
High Speed EKTACHROME, Daylight Type (EH)	Color Slides	160	Daylight or Blue Flash	135-20, 135-36, 126-20, 120
High Speed EKTACHROME, Type B (EHB)	Color Slides	125	Photolamp (3200 K) or Existing Tungsten Light	135-20, 136-36, 120
KODACOLOR-X (CX)	Color Prints	80	Daylight or Blue Flash	135-20, 135-36, 126-12, 126-20, 828, 127, 620, 120, 616, 116

Above all, set out with the goal of making the best possible pictures. *Seeing* the best picture subject is often more important than the mechanics of handling various cameras, films, and other apparatus. You can do this with increasing skill and pride if you take your time in choosing camera angles, in deciding on one subject to be the center of interest, and then concentrating on composition around it. Before taking a picture, view the scene through your camera's viewfinder, and ask yourself:

1. Precisely what do I want to show?
2. Is this the most interesting point of view for photographing this subject?
3. Do any foreground or background objects spoil my picture?
4. What objects can I omit and still tell my story?

Once you set out for the parks, start to tell your story, whether in movies or stills, in a sequence. This pattern will help you organize your pictures with continuity and to make them more interesting. A few shots of how you travel are appropriate—through the windshield of your car or from the window of an airplane, for example. You can minimize the effects of camera movement in pictures made from any moving vehicle by using a wide-angle lens or the wide-angle position of your zoom lens. When traveling on land, shoot in the direction the vehicle is moving rather than at right angles to it. You may want to keep a log, numbering individual exposures roll by roll, with matching notes and the names and addresses of people you meet to whom you want to send pictures.

There are some types of subjects you'll want to photograph at each park you visit. For example, each national park has a title sign at the entrance, which provides a logical title picture for the sequence. You could personalize your pictures by photographing one member of your family greeting the ranger at the gateway. One of your first important stops should then be at the park Visitor Center for a real introduction to the values and meaning of the park through the museum displays, slide presentations, and movies they present. Here you can take pictures of dioramas, relief models, and oil paintings. Photographers find these to be outstanding subjects reflecting park themes; they are best taken with flash or with the camera on a tripod, using time-exposure technique. When you take flash pictures, avoid distracting reflections in your pictures by shooting at an angle to shiny surfaces such as glass. A ranger-naturalist will answer any of your questions, including those dealing with photography. You can also purchase natural-history guides that interpret biology, botany, geology, the whole park environment. The Visitor Center will show you how to look at the land—the plant associations, life zones and life communities, how to trace the story of ecological succession—and thus to photograph it with meaning and feeling.

In the parks of the Southwest, for instance, a dying juniper reveals the character and personality of an arid region. A pothole full of water demonstrates how precious and determined life can be. A flash flood unfolds the fury to which the land has been subjected for centuries. In the Northwest and in the Great Smoky Mountains, fog and rain will give mood to pictures and understanding of the nourishment bestowed by moisture to the great forests.

A photographer takes the weather in the parks as it comes and makes the most of it, as nature does. Bright sunlight is best for distant mountain vistas, but there are dramatic effects in storm clouds. Pictures of mountains can be aided by cross-lighting, plus a foreground object, such as a plant or person. A skylight filter may help remove excess bluishness from distant scenes and subjects on overcast days or in open shade, but should not be used with sunlit people in the near foreground. With simple nonadjustable still cameras, you can take color pictures in bright or hazy sunlight—as long as you can see fairly sharp shadows. More advanced still cameras and movie cameras (even the least expensive) have faster lenses, which enable you also to shoot pictures on cloudy days and in shade and other dark situations. Overcast days are excellent for wildflowers, with light diffused and shadows softened. For shooting rainy-day close-ups, consider a clear plastic umbrella to protect the camera and yet allow light to reach the subject.

Plants and flowers are among the attractive photographic subjects you'll find at almost all national parks. A whole hillside carpeted with wildflowers is striking in itself, but with a close-up lens you can fill your picture with a single plant, blossom, or petal. Flowers are mostly found in spring, but plants are ever-changing, from dawn to dusk, from one season to the next, and never without form and beauty waiting to be recorded. They are found in unexpected places: at the edge of a receding glacier, representing the first stages of plant succession; across the floor of the seemingly barren desert; mosses and lichens spreading over massive boulders, with delicate blossoms all their own, and patient determination to transform rock into soil.

You can show plants and flowers in their environment and the details of their blooms and foliage by making a sequence including distant, medium, and finally close-up shots. On extreme close-ups, don't forget that the camera lens and viewfinder don't see quite the same subject area (unless you're using a single-lens reflex camera), because the viewfinder and the lens are slightly separated. To correct for this phenomenon, called parallax, tip the camera slightly in the direction of the viewfinder—the closer to the subject, the more you need to tip. Some serious photographers take along an old blanket or piece of canvas to lie on while photographing subjects close to the ground. When photographing shaded subjects, you can sometimes throw light into shadow areas by using a simple reflector made from metal foil or white paper or cloth. If possible, plan your flower shooting for early morning, when the problem of blossoms bobbing in the wind usually is minimized. Remember that some expert photographers spend a whole day shooting two or three flowers, observing, absorbing, and admiring the full setting of soil, water, climate, and interwoven web of life. And always, in the spirit of the national parks, they leave them for others to enjoy.

Patience is even more of a must in photographing the wildlife that abounds in the parks. Animals roaming free in their native habitat are great photographic subjects, but wild animals are where you find them—not in any set, predictable place. They move about because of season, time of day, weather, availability of food, and other reasons they have chosen not to disclose. National parks are meant for wildlife on their own terms; the parks are not like zoos, where animals are contained within a definite area. Some knowledge of wildlife habits will help you find the animals, and so will a pair of good binoculars. The best approach is to rise with the sun and to hike early in the morning through forests and meadows. By eight or nine A.M. many mammals are in seclusion, not to be seen again until evening, when they come out into open areas to feed. Trying to get an animal's attention is a mistake, especially when the subject is dangerous and may charge—as it has every right to do on its own grounds. The wiser tack is to follow from a distance with telephoto lens and sheer patience. Feeding, hunting, killing, wounding, frightening, or capturing of any bird or animal is prohibited in a national park. So is use or display of firearms, which must be declared at the entry station.

You'll do well to concentrate your photographic attention on nature. Pictures of waterfalls and mountains can be improved by the inclusion of people in colorful clothing, but don't get people in settings inharmonious with nature—like the father who foolishly tried to pose his small child astride a black bear.

There are plenty of park scenes in which people fit logically, especially in camp life, with mother cooking breakfast on the gasoline stove or father and the children putting up the tent. Try to have your subjects wear their brightest clothing to add color to your pictures, and take pictures of your subjects doing things so they don't stare self-consciously at the camera. For example, there's a chance to tell a complete picture story in fishing, from tying trout flies at home, renting the boat, casting, making the strike, and finally frying the fish over campfire coals.

You can give a special touch to pictures by "framing" them in your own way with materials you like best. Natural frames add a feeling of depth to a picture and keep the viewer's attention concentrated on the picture within. You can use an overhanging branch, a gnarled juniper, or a brace of cactus blossom in the foreground to frame your picture. Keep the frame at least five feet from the camera so that frame *and* scene are in focus.

The national parks have relatively few rules and regulations, considering the tremendous number of visitors they receive and the need to protect the natural resource for present and future generations. Most rules involve courtesy and common sense.

For instance, if you're driving, viewpoints and turn-offs provide the best places to stop in safety and take pictures. Whenever you stop for a picture, pull completely off the road.

Stay on the marked trails. It's not only destructive to the terrain to wander astray, but in some parks it can be hazardous.

Because heat and humidity spoil film, you should avoid leaving loaded cameras and film in direct sunlight anywhere in your car, and particularly not in hot trunks or glove compartments. Use your prepaid processing mailers to lighten your load as you travel.

As soon as possible on arrival home, put your slides in order, edit your movies, or put your prints in an album. If you delay, you may never do it properly. You may want to number all your slides to help you keep them in an orderly sequence. Avoid showing pictures that are fuzzy, too dark, too light, or just plain uninteresting. Instead, make a dry run of your show and pick the very best you've got. When you show slides or movies, have the screen set up and the projector focused and ready to go before your guests arrive.

Keep your program shorter than an hour, and you'll give your friends the thrill the national parks have given to you.

AMERICA'S NATIONAL PARKS

Acadia National Park
Bar Harbor, Maine 04609

The first national park in the East (established 1919), and the only one in New England, typifies the rugged, rocky coast of Maine. It covers only 41,634 acres, but its surf-splashed cliffs rise to the highest point along the Atlantic Coast. In the interior, deep blue lakes shielded by steep slopes are vestiges of ancient glacial action.

Photographic subjects range from bays and harbors speckled in summer with sails of pleasure boats and the sea roaring against the rocks to hundreds of varieties of wildflowers in the cool mountain forests. Birds are varied. Most visitors come in summer, when the naturalist program of guided walks, lectures, and other services is in full operation, but spring and autumn are pleasant too. Bring warm clothes and raincoat, for nights are cool and you can count on rain in any season. Acadia lies forty-seven miles southeast of Bangor.

Picture-Taking Stops

Bar Harbor, the gateway to the park and largest settlement on Mount Desert Island, still retains the flavor of old fishing days around the docks. You can get a picture of your own family on a deep-sea-fishing trip or aboard the celebrated "Bluenose," the international motor ferry that runs daily during summer to Yarmouth, Nova Scotia. Starting from Bar Harbor, the *Frenchman Bay Cruise,* conducted by the National Park Service, provides a wonderful two-hour swing by sea around Frenchman Bay and the Cranberry Islands. Champlain sailed this way on his 1604 exploration of the French province of Acadia. You can take many excellent shots of the islands, wildlife, caves, and seacoast—and get the benefit of the naturalist lecture.

Many of Acadia's focal points are linked by the park-loop road. At *Anemone Cave,* waves at work have tunneled eighty-five feet into the granite cliffs. Pools glisten from a profusion of rockweed, algae, kelp, flowerlike anemone, and dog whelk. The cave is best photographed in the morning and at low tide, with flash for the cave interior and this marine life. *Sand Beach,* a sweeping arc along the ocean, is also best in early morning, when you are

12

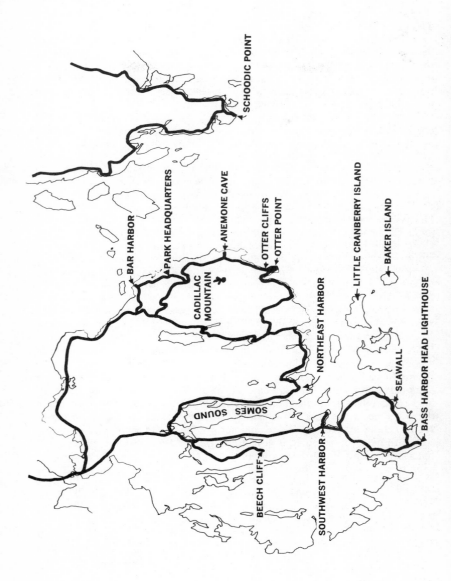

SCHOODIC POINT

BAR HARBOR
PARK HEADQUARTERS
ANEMONE CAVE
OTTER CLIFFS
OTTER POINT

CADILLAC
MOUNTAIN

NORTHEAST HARBOR

SOMES SOUND

LITTLE CRANBERRY ISLAND

BAKER ISLAND

SEAWALL

BASS HARBOR HEAD LIGHTHOUSE

BEECH CLIFF

SOUTHWEST HARBOR

13

likely to get it in its natural state with black-and-white guillemots diving for fish. *Thunder Hole* is especially recommended for movies. When the waves and tides are right (usually low tide), the sea rushes into this narrow chasm with a resounding splash. *Otter Cliffs* provides a fine chance to photograph the family with huge rocks and sea or coastline in the background. From the area above the cliffs you can photograph rocks and waves framed with branches of spruce trees. *Otter Point* continues the beauty of Otter Cliffs. The nature trail winds through spruce and fir to the shore, where wild roses meet the salt spray. *Cadillac Mountain* is the highest point on the East Coast. Magnificent vistas unfold at the horizon. Close at hand you can walk the nature trail and photograph the scene where massive sheets of glacial ice gouged lakes and shaved peaks to bare granite.

Continuing on the loop road, *Northeast Harbor* affords another good chance for harbor and boat pictures. Offshore, cormorants and gulls flock around a rocky shoal, while small lobster boats are seen hauling in their "pots." *Isleford Museum* is accessible on a cruise from Northeast Harbor. You'll have a fine opportunity for shots where great fishing fleets once whitened the horizon with hundreds of sails. When you reach the historical museum on Little Cranberry Island, use flash to photograph old ship anchors and lobster pots. *Baker Island* is also reached by sea cruise from Northeast Harbor. A ranger-naturalist will explain points of interest en route—he's a good personality to work into a picture story. On Baker Island, shoot the Coast Guard lighthouse and huge blocks of granite tossed up by winter storms. Somesville, the site of Mount Desert Island's first permanent settlement (1761), lies on the loop road at the head of a steep-sided fjord called *Somes Sound*, providing a scene quite comparable with those of Norway. *Beech Cliff*, several miles south of Somesville, is reached on a five-minute walk through a spruce-fir forest. It overlooks Echo Lake for a breathtaking view of water, beach, mountains, and fir forests. Carry your camera to make panoramic pictures of the lake and beach area.

Southwest Harbor is one of the old fishing settlements from the days when schooners and brigs were built in every cove. It still retains much of the old flavor. In such villages you can photograph interesting craft pieces, including hand-carved birds on driftwood bases. *Seawall* derives its name from the jumbled rocks piled along the shore by storm waves between the loop road and the sea. One of the park's two campgrounds is located here. Campfire programs held every evening during summer are illustrated with color slides designed to help you enjoy your visit more. *Bass Harbor Head Lighthouse*, at the southernmost tip of the island, is best photographed from a low angle to capture the white lighthouse against the blue sky. *Bass Harbor* typifies the tiny down-east boating villages. Use flash inside the Bass Harbor Country Store to photograph the interesting and unique equipment used by Maine fishermen of a century ago. Photograph the sign over the door as a title for your picture story recounting the adventure of your family exploring the maritime past. *Schoodic Point*, about an hour and a half by car from Bar Harbor around Frenchman Bay, is a relatively isolated—but truly outstanding—part of the park. The shore is rimmed by a park road, and you can get wonderful pictures of sea and pounding surf.

Big Bend National Park
Texas 79834

The masterpiece of Chihuahuan desert landscape, covering 708,221 acres along the Texas-Mexico border, is dominated by the upthrust of the Chisos Mountains. Giant *arroyos* and imposing gorges are spread through the area. Crags, canyons, and rocky spires present a pattern of contrasting color and grandeur of the wilderness frontier. The Rio Grande makes its gigantic curve—the big bend—while forming 107 miles of park boundary and carving three deep and dramatic canyons out of limestone rock.

Millions of years ago the entire Big Bend area was submerged by an ocean. Sediments of mud, sand, and lime spread across the floor of the sea later hardened into rock. Various types of shells and fish life were fossilized in forming the rock, and traces are still found embedded over the area. Then came volcanic action in the earth's interior, causing the surface to uplift and waters to recede. Now erosion has carved a cross-section out of the earth, etching the rocks of different geological eras in bold relief.

The park contains more than one thousand different plants, including rare species found only here. There is a wide range of fauna—at least 240 species of birds, and 67 kinds of mammals, from small rodents to coyote, ringtails, javelina, the sleek pronghorn, and mountain lion. Big Bend is about four hundred miles west of San Antonio and three hundred miles southeast of El Paso.

Picture-Taking Stops

Approaching from the east through Marathon (thirty-nine miles away), *Persimmon Gap*, a low pass near the entrance, has been a landmark for many years, part of the route of the Great Comanche War Trail. Drive leisurely—you'll see more and get a better variety of pictures. Wildflowers are found along the roads in the park in almost every month of the year, but desert blossom reaches its peak from late February through April. Signs along the improved gravel road to *Dagger Flat* identify many plants. You drive through a rare spectacle of thousands of huge giant dagger yucca *(Yucca carnerosana)*, unfolding massive clusters of creamy blossoms.

Continuing on the main road, the *Fossil Bone Exhibit* near Tornillo Creek displays bones of an extinct mammal, the Coryphodon, found embedded in sandstone and dating from the period when dinosaurs and giant crocodiles roamed through dark marshes and tropical forests. *Tornillo Flats* is one of the most likely places for wildlife, especially at the beginning and end of the day. Tornillo, which means "screw" in Spanish, incidentally, here refers to the interesting Screwbean Mesquite, marked by spiral-shaped pods, well worth a close-up picture.

Park headquarters, an attractive low building that blends into the landscape, lies at Panther Junction. Turning west by car, you can observe the vegetation change while climbing from desert into the woodlands of the *Chisos Basin*, center of activity most of the year, with campground, store, concession-operated cottages and lodge. Illustrated talks are given most evenings

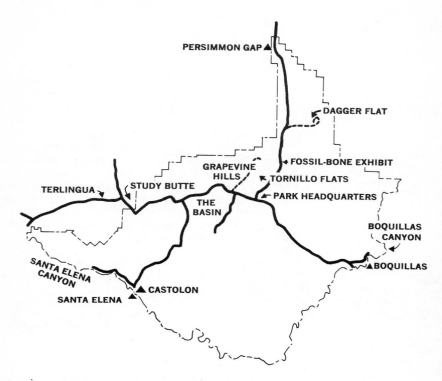

throughout the year. From here you'll be able to take the one-fourth-mile Window View Trail to photograph the great gap in the mountains called the *Window*, passing colorful formations along the way. Sunset spreading across the lower plains makes an excellent photo study through the Window.

With Chisos Basin as headquarters, you can set forth to explore and photograph highlights of the park. Take a one-day trip to *Santa Elena Canyon*, forty-seven miles away. Early morning is the best time; sun strikes the canyon walls just right for picture-taking, but by noon there is little or no sunlight in the canyon. Watch for an abandoned ranch down in a clump of trees on the west side of the road. Here you can sit quietly and photograph birds feeding and nesting. You can get excellent pictures of the Mule Ears and other rugged formations in the wilderness area to the south, Tuff Canyon to the west, and Cerro Castolon, a landmark along the Rio Grande. The old frontier military outpost of *Castolon* will be a highspot of the trip. You will want to visit and photograph the store, occupying a building erected by the Army in 1919 as a barracks, and now a living museum. The river is so narrow here that you can cross by ferry (a rowboat) to the little Mexican farming village of Santa Elena, with many old adobe and stone houses. Get a photo of your family picnicking at the mouth of the canyon on the U.S. side. From the picnic area a footpath leads into the heart of the canyon, revealing the immensity of its 1,500-foot-high walls.

Another photo tour should be made to *Boquillas Canyon*, the longest of Big Bend's famous gorges, located thirty-five miles from the basin, past Rio

Grande Village, which includes a campground, store, and trailer facilities suited for winter use (when it grows cool at Chisos Basin). You can have a fine time crossing the border aboard a burro, handled by a friendly Mexican lad, into isolated Boquillas pueblo, where the proud, humble people will treat you with respect if you accord the same to them. This is a late-afternoon trip. Be sure to be well out of the canyon to get the full effect of sun emblazoning the canyon walls before sunset.

The day-long horseback ride to the *South Rim* is an outstanding experience. You can make a picture sequence following the change in vegetation with rising elevation, upward from piñon, oak, and juniper life communities to an "island forest in the sky." Atop the South Rim, 7,200 feet above sea level, perpendicular cliffs drop more than a thousand feet to the lower Chisos. You'll get pictures of spectacular vistas unfolding across the Rio Grande into Old Mexico. Another good trip is the four-mile round-trip hike on *Lost Mine Trail* from the basin to Lost Mine Peak, overlooking ridges and valleys, with a breathtaking vista from the top. You may see a tarantula. Look him over respectfully and photograph him from a distance; he will bother you far less than you can bother him.

If you leave the park through the west entrance, you can take pictures at the mining ghost towns of *Terlingua* and *Study Butte* en route to the scenic Camino del Rio and Presidio, a gateway into Mexico.

Bryce Canyon National Park
Bryce Canyon, Utah 84717

Few places in the world provide a better opportunity to perceive the power and persistence of earth-shaping forces than this photographer's paradise of southern Utah. Within 36,010 acres, the geology of the last sixty million years is laid bare. It began with layers of sediment deposited by inland lakes and seas, followed by mountain building and inevitable erosion. Rain, alternate frost and thaw, running water, plant roots forcing themselves into the cracks, and chemicals in the air have altered rock formations and produced new ones.

This kaleidoscope of color ranges from pink and iron-red to cream, here and there striped with lavender and blue, spreading out from the amphitheaterlike rim as far as the eye can see. Many of the fantastic spires and pinnacles are named. Others invite the imagination and interpretation of the camera to suggest apt new titles.

Picture-Taking Stops

Your first view over the plateau rim will come as you approach from the north, possibly from Zion National Park and Cedar Breaks National Monument. Several excellent overlooks are located along the rim drive or require only short walks on paved trails. Combine these stops with hiking or riding for close-ups of the formations. Telephoto and wide-angle lenses will be of great help. It's generally easier to get the most dramatic pictures during early-morning and late-afternoon hours, when incandescent effects of great beauty are possible. Indeed, every serious photographer should experience at least one sunrise at Bryce Canyon, since most viewpoints on the rim face to the east. If you use an exposure meter, take a reading of the sky—this will give proper color to the sky and silhouette foreground objects. With an automatic or nonadjustable camera, just aim and shoot. Afternoon summer thunderstorms are common and also offer dramatic possibilities.

The first overlook, *Fairyland View*, is a good spot to try some pictures with side-lighting and back-lighting. This is the starting point of the 5 1/2-mile Fairyland loop trail, not especially steep but a good all-day hike with unlimited scenery of Fairyland, brilliantly colored Tower Bridge (so named because it resembles the famous bridge across the Thames in London), and other features awaiting the imaginative photographer. A little farther south, still close to the park entrance, the *Bryce Canyon Visitor Center* provides orientation exhibits in geology, biology, botany, and archaeology.

Now take to the other overlooks and trails. But follow a leisurely pace in this high country, eight to nine thousand feet above sea level, allowing extra time for everything. At *Sunrise Point*, walk down the trail a short distance and shoot south toward Sunset Point during the morning hours. For an early-morning back-lighted scene, walk to the south along the rim trail and face east. Both of these also make good midday shots, especially in summer. At Sunset Point, overlooking the heart of the Bryce Amphitheater, you can join the naturalist-led walk over the Navajo Loop, the most popular hike in the park (about 1 1/2 miles and 1 1/2 hours), starting at nine A.M. each summer morning. It begins with a gradual 521-foot descent into the canyon, then winds among an outstanding array of formations in the amphitheater, with time for rest and picture-taking.

At *Inspiration Point,* you look directly down Bryce Creek to the east and Silent City to the northeast, with an endless variety of sculptures. *Bryce Point* affords a choice location for a panoramic view. Follow the trail about one hundred yards from the parking lot and you will be almost surrounded by the scene below. The main features to shoot are Goblin's Grotto, the Wall of Windows, and the Alligator. The spectacular Natural Bridge is so close to the road that a wide-angle lens is necessary to encompass the entire formation. Bear in mind that the deep blue of the sky makes the coloring of the rocks appear more intense. But don't neglect the possibility of filling your whole picture area with rock formations, omitting the sky altogether. Deep shadows may turn up, but even if they're black they will add drama to your pictures.

North from *Rainbow Point,* more of the escarpment can be seen than from any other viewpoint. High to the northeast are the Table Cliffs, capped by the pink Wasatch Formation, and even farther, the Henry Mountains are visible on clear days. *Yovimpa Point,* the southernmost overlook in the park, is the only one with a wide view directly to the south, affording an unparalleled vista of the Kaibab Plateau area, including the North Rim of the Grand Canyon. Here you can catch the setting sun's rays on the Pink Cliffs.

If you come in late spring or early summer, before the heavy travel season, wildflowers alone will make your trip worthwhile. You can see and photograph the delicate star lily, wallflower, primrose, paintbrush, columbine, yarrow, and penstemon. The Utah state flower, the white-petaled cuplike sego lily, puts on a fine display, generally in July. But let it not be forgotten among photographers that the park is a year-round happening and is truly spectacular after a fresh snowfall when storm clouds scatter and the sun comes through. Skies then are deep blue, haze-free; the snow sparkles on the delicate formations and accentuates the color. Winter is an excellent opportunity for picture-taking in the national parks. During winter, roads are kept open to four major viewpoints: Sunset, Inspiration, Bryce, and Paria View.

Canyonlands National Park
Moab, Utah 84532

Surrounding the confluence of two great rivers of the West, the Green and Colorado, are deep, winding cliffs of orange-red sandstone, towering spires, arches, needles, and bold mesas—a wilderness environment. This new national park, established in 1964, embraces 257,640 acres of flaming color and rocky landscape.

Travel is limited in the park, but expert professional guides in Moab and Monticello offer trips into the immense back country by four-wheel-drive vehicles, boat, horseback, and on foot. But even the casual visitor can get a generous introduction, and plenty of photographs, in a two-wheel-drive vehicle. Two approaches (both graded dirt roads) are available to passenger cars. The road from the northern gateway, the old pioneer town of Moab, leads to the Island in the Sky district. From the southeast gateway, Monticello, another road brings motorists into the spectacular Needles district, with thousands of red-and-white rounded pillars, spires, and balanced rocks. Canyonlands, still lightly visited, gives one the feeling of true Western wilderness.

Picture-Taking Stops

The Island in the Sky is a great plateau ringed by sheer cliffs. As you approach from Moab, stop first at *Mesa Trail* arch, where a one-fourth-mile trail leads to this small scenic arch in the east rim. The best times for taking pictures are very early in the morning and in the afternoon; the best angle is looking southeast. *Grandview Point,* the tip of the mesa dominating the land between the two rivers, affords spectacular rimrock views. You can drive to the point in a passenger car and get outstanding pictures anytime except around noon. However, it's best to shoot Monument Basin, with its red-hued cliffs and standing rocks, in the morning. Haze sometimes makes pictures of the Needles impossible. *Green River Overlook,* on the south rim of the northwestern finger of the island mesa, offers excellent views of the White Rim, including the Turk's Head and Murphy Hogback and a portion of the wild Green River. The best times for pictures are midmorning and early afternoon; the best angle is southwest. At the end of a short hiking trail, *Upheaval Dome,* a deep, vertical-walled crater with a cream-colored mass of salted stone thrust upward through surrounding sandstone, will be a highspot to record. You can get pictures from the Whale Rock trail in the morning, at any angle to the west, and from the Dome trail at any hours *except* early morning and noon. You can hike much of Upheaval Dome, but let a ranger know you're going and allow plenty of time; the trip is rough and the return all uphill.

The photographer who takes to the *White Rim* jeep road will find many rewarding subjects. Starting on the east side, Musselman Arch, an arch formed in the sandstone, should be shot with a wide-angle lens to get a full view. You can shoot inward from the rim to the Island in the Sky, at such landmarks as Washerwoman Arch; the best time is midmorning, and the best angle is looking slightly southwest from where the arch first comes into view.

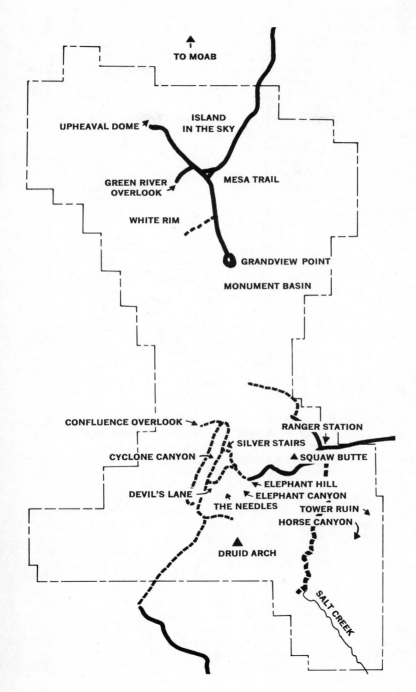

TO MOAB

UPHEAVAL DOME

ISLAND
IN THE SKY

GREEN RIVER
OVERLOOK

MESA TRAIL

WHITE RIM

GRANDVIEW POINT

MONUMENT BASIN

CONFLUENCE OVERLOOK

RANGER STATION

SILVER STAIRS

CYCLONE CANYON

SQUAW BUTTE

ELEPHANT HILL

DEVIL'S LANE

ELEPHANT CANYON

THE NEEDLES

TOWER RUIN

HORSE CANYON

DRUID ARCH

SALT CREEK

Monument Basin, directly below, between the rim and the Colorado River, offers innumerable subjects among the sandstone-capped stone figures. Best times are midmorning and early afternoon; two of the best positions are looking south at the northernmost end of the basin and at the western end, where the White Rim road leaves the basin, looking east at the unmistakable Totem Pole. On the west side of the Island in the Sky, *Candlestick Tower,* isolated from the mesa, offers good pictures from the east in the morning, from the west in the afternoon.

In the *Needles District,* you can drive a passenger car over a graded dirt road to Elephant Hill, but you can cover much more in four-wheel-drive, on a pack trip, or on foot. Remember that there are plenty of drive-through parks everywhere—Canyonland is frontier country to challenge the spirit and skill. The *Cave Spring Ranger Station* is a good place to learn about road conditions. Three miles beyond are Squaw Spring and the Squaw Flat campground, from where a footpath leads into the spectacular Needles area. From Elephant Hill (another three miles), the jeep road continues across *Elephant Canyon,* with rapidly changing scenery in all directions. It is about 3 1/2 miles to Devil's Pocket, with its overhanging rocks (best shot in morning or afternoon). Continuing from there to Devil's Lane, you will be able to see Indian ruins and pictographs. From the entrance to Devil's Lane it is about four miles to *Chesler Park,* ringed by thousands of red-and-white pillars, spires, and balanced rocks, some rising as high as thirty-story buildings. From Chesler Park there is a foot trail to Druid Arch, the climax of Elephant Canyon (best shot in the morning); it is a spectacular hike.

After seeing and photographing Devil's Pocket, Devil's Lane, Chesler Park, the Indian pictographs, Druid Arch, and the Needles, you can return to the junction of the road at the entrance to Devil's Lane and take the other fork to the north, leading down over the Silver Stairs to the Confluence Overlook, and you can photograph the merger of two mighty rivers, their differing shades of silt-laden waters, and the wildness they carry from the high country of the West into the heart of the Canyonlands. Then turn south through Cyclone Canyon into the fantasy of the Grabens, parallel sunken valleys where sandstone looks different from what you have previously photographed.

You can get another perspective by starting due south from Cave Spring Ranger Station (again by jeep) along *Salt Creek* for three miles, then turning east into *Horse Canyon* for such spectacular sights as Tower Ruin, Key Hole Ruin, and Paul Bunyan's Potty. Then return to the main valley and continue up Horse Canyon, where Indian ruins are visible in the cliffs on both sides to the sharp-eyed viewer. Beyond the Narrows, a designated viewpoint opens on a rugged wild canyon crowned with Castle Arch at the summit. When you return to the Horse Canyon-Salt Creek junction, turn south on Salt Creek for a distance of nine miles to Angel Arch Canyon, where a spectacular sandstone bridge is guarded by an angel-like figure. These environs were discovered and named as recently as 1955. Because Angel Arch is best photographed in early morning, you may want to stay overnight at the primitive campsite at the foot of the canyon, continue south through the Jump to photograph the All-American Man, with seven-thousand-foot-high Cedar Mesa in the background.

For complete coverage, you may want to photograph the Canyonlands from the river. Approximately ninety-five miles of the Green and Colorado are within the park, and boat tours are run frequently. Cataract Canyon, below the river junction, is known as "the explorers' nightmare and modern river-runner's challenge."

Carlsbad Caverns
Carlsbad, New Mexico 88220

Renowned for beauty and immensity, the chambers of Carlsbad Caverns—the most photographed caves in the world—reach more than a thousand feet deep beneath the foothills of the Guadalupe Mountains. The limestones began to form two hundred million years ago from organic life on a barrier reef bordering an inland sea. The caverns were hollowed out by underground water slowly dissolving through cracks in the earth.

The formations of limestone are of endless variety and beauty, patiently formed by seepage of rainwater and snowmelt. Over centuries this process has produced stalactites, stalagmites, columns and pillars of many sizes, shapes, and colors. One formation poised over the path in the Big Room is aptly named Sword of Damocles and is followed by totempoles, snowbanked forests, the celebrated Rock of Ages, and the Giant Dome.

Late in the last century, valuable deposits of bat guano were discovered and mined in the caves. One young miner, James L. White, explored deeply and brought the underground treasures to public attention, and the Carlsbad Caverns were set aside for preservation and public enjoyment in 1923. Development has been limited to the largest, most accessible portions down to the 829-foot level. These are reached either by elevator or a natural entrance on foot. The town of Carlsbad lies twenty-seven miles north of the park and El Paso, Texas, about one hundred and fifty miles west.

Picture-Taking Stops

The first scenic turnoff on the seven-mile entrance road is approximately four miles inside the park. A short nature trail leads past well-labeled plants of the Chihuahuan Desert. Spring is the most colorful time, with red claretcup, yellow prickly pear, purble verbena, red-trimmed ocotillo. One mile farther, a turnoff overlooks the rugged scenery of the canyon below and, another quarter mile, a pull-off features a short trail leading to an even better view of Walnut Canyon.

The *Visitor Center,* at the end of the seven-mile drive, is an excellent photo stop. On one side are the picturesque stone residences of employees (which many visitors mistake for Indian ruins). On the other side lies the vast Delaware Basin in Texas. On a clear day one can see Guadalupe Peak, the highest point in Texas. A three-story observation tower atop the Visitor Center provides the best view of these features.

There are three ways of touring underground, where most pictures are taken:

Cavern Tour is divided in two parts. The first half, lasting an hour and three-quarters, starts at the natural entrance down steep switch-back trails to a depth of 829 feet, then rises 80 feet into the underground lunchroom. This portion passes through the Green Lake Room, named for a small green pool; the ornate King's Palace, with curtains of glittering cave onyx; and the Queen's Chamber, adorned with translucent formations. On this first part,

23

flash and time photography are not permitted, since flashbulbs and tripods can be hazardous on steep trails. After lunch, this group joins the Big Room Tour.

Big Room Tour begins in the Visitor Center, descending by elevator from the lobby to the underground lunchroom, 750 feet below, which opens directly to the Big Room itself, the vast chamber where the ceiling arches 255 feet overhead. The tour takes about two hours and covers 1 1/4 miles over mostly level trail. During all but the summer months, this is a guided tour, with the same photo restrictions as the first portion. However, every afternoon in fall, winter, and spring a special photo tour is offered. It passes around a part of the Big Room, stopping wherever the visitors wish to photograph. Time permitting, the tour also visits the four scenic rooms which lie on the route of the first part of the regular tour.

Semi-Guided Tour of the Big Room is offered during the three summer months. Visitors may enter at any time and walk through at their own pace. Guides are stationed throughout to answer questions. Photos may be taken at will, the sole restriction being that visitors stay on the trail for their own safety and protection of the priceless cave features. All tours end with an elevator ride to the Visitor Center.

Principal photo features in the Big Room:

Hall of the Giants	Mirror Lake
Giant Dome	Grape Arbor
Temple of the Sun	Crystal Spring Dome
Santa Claus	Rock of Ages
Totempole	Twin Domes

Three hundred yards from the Visitor Center is the amphitheater for the evening bat-flight program. During the summer months hundreds of thousands of Mexican freetail bats spiral out of the natural entrance to feed on night-flying beetles and moths, affording exceptional opportunities for motion-picture photographers.

Crater Lake National Park
Crater Lake, Oregon 97604

The deepest lake in the United States is colored a deep and brilliant blue, due to its ability to return blue rays of sunlight from the clear depths of 1,932 feet. The lake is framed with evergreen forests of pine, fir, and hemlock, typical of the high Cascades. There could hardly be anything more fitting for the nature photographer.

Once, ages ago, Mount Mazama, a twelve-thousand-foot volcanic peak, rose on this site. It erupted and literally "blew its top," so that Mazama pumice and fine dust were blown hundreds of miles to the north and east. An immense basin was left, twenty square miles in area, surrounded by towering walls. Cradled in the extinct volcano, the entire lake can be taken in by the eye at one time from the rim of lava cliffs.

There are numerous locations for good views of prominent cinder cones and countless lake views. When seeking to take pictures from precarious perches, you should be extremely careful of loose volcanic rock and the rolling pumice underfoot. One cameraman at the turn of the century, who came to shoot some of the first winter views of Crater Lake, has not been seen since, although his camera and tripod were found the next spring. The south entrance is forty-six miles from Klamath Falls, the north entrance ninety-two miles from Bend, and the west entrance sixty-nine miles from Medford.

Picture-Taking Stops

Approaching from the west, the sign designating the park boundary is in a forest of hemlocks, western white pines, and Shasta red firs, an instant signal that there is far more than the lake itself to appreciate within the 160,290 acres of the national park. *Castle Creek Canyon,* two hundred and fifty feet deep, is marked by vertical columns, deposited by glowing avalanches of pumice, followed by scoria, that raced down the mountain as part of the dramatic sequence in the destruction of Mount Mazama. A short distance farther, *Whitehorse Creek* drops two hundred and fifty feet in less than a mile, rushing through the spectacular gorge of Llao's Hallway. The chasm walls are close enough to be spanned by outstretched arms.

After passing Annie Spring campground, bear south as far as *Godfrey Glen,* a distance of 1.4 miles, one of the key features of the park apart from the lake. The canyon floor, two hundred feet below, expands into a grassy park; you may get pictures of black-tailed deer roaming along the stream. The dark-gray scoria walls are pierced by spiny columns, fossil fumaroles marking the site of rising hot gases associated with the downrush of Mazama's glowing avalanches. Now double back and head for the rim, stopping at *Castle Crest,* just past park headquarters, where wildflowers are identified by plant labels. Flowers of the high mountains appear late and disappear early, but in late summer bright berries of Pacific red elder gleam along the roadway, while phlox, knotweed, and red Lewis monkeyflowers continue in their brilliance.

The flower exhibit at the Visitor Center in Rim Village will help you to identify plants you will want to photograph. The broad terrace of *Sinnott Memorial*, located right on the lake front outside the exhibit building, is an excellent orientation and photo point, where talks on the origin of the lake are given several times daily. From here drive clockwise around the lake for a continuing array of outstanding scenery on the thirty-three-mile drive. Absolute calmness with glasslike conditions for perfect reflection on the lake is not unusual. However, concession-operated launches operate mid-June through Labor Day from nine A.M. to four-thirty P.M. Perfect reflections, therefore, must be obtained before or after those hours.

From the viewpoint at *Discovery Point* you will have an impressive vantage over Wizard Island, which is actually a small volcanic cone of red, brown, and black fragments produced on the lake bottom by seething fire after destruction of Mazama. You may want a picture of one of your family reading the interpretive marker which relates how John Wesley Hillman discovered Crater Lake in 1853; he called it the Deep Blue Lake. Continuing on Rim Drive, *Union Peak* viewpoint furnishes a good view to the west and south of forests, volcanic peaks, and distant mountains, including Mount Shasta in California on crystal-clear days. The *Watchman* viewpoint also affords good pictures of Wizard Island. An 0.8-mile trail from the parking area leads to the fire lookout station on the summit, with excellent views in all directions.

When you reach the junction with the north entrance road, take a side trip of several miles past the Red Cone into the *Pumice Desert*, produced by volcanic forces. Try to interpret through pictures the struggle of individual lodgepole pines to gain a foothold and to fulfill their mission in the story of plant succession by clothing devastation with a new forest. Then return to the Rim Drive and *Cleetwood Cove*, an especially good point for photographing the striking blue color of the lake water. Cleetwood Trail is the only access to the water and to the starting point of launch trips, highly recommended for photographers. The trail is only 1.1 miles, but allow plenty of time, and don't carry any more gear than you need—it is steep going down, and steeper on the uphill return. You'll get tremendous picture opportunities on the 2 1/2-hour *launch trip*. Besides the scenics, if you heed the naturalist's lecture on board, you'll get unusual pictures of Wizard Island and the unique dike remnant called Phantom Ship, and other expressions of geologic action, and be able to interpret them.

Continuing around the lake to the east side, take the short spur to *Cloudcap*, where the Rim Drive reaches its highest point. Not only are there excellent lake vistas, but weathered whitebark pines at hand are particularly striking, part of the determined plant community that endures bright sun during the day and freezing temperature almost every night of the year. Look closely at the ground and you will see rare vegetative life forms, like the pumice grapefern, which lifts its solitary frond gracefully a mere two inches above the pumice. Hikers may want to follow the 2 1/2-mile trail, on a fairly gentle grade, to the fire tower at the summit of *Mount Scott*, the highest point in the park. With wide-angle lens you can get a panorama of the entire lake.

Once again on the Rim Drive, *Castle Rock* viewpoint provides the best angle for shooting the geological oddity called Castle Rock on the caldera wall, complete with stratified orange and apricot towers, against a background of the lake and Mount Thielsen in the distance. At *Kerr Notch*, one of the lowest points on the rim (577 feet above the lake), the view framing Phantom Ship and Dutton Cliff through the trees is one of the choicest for telling

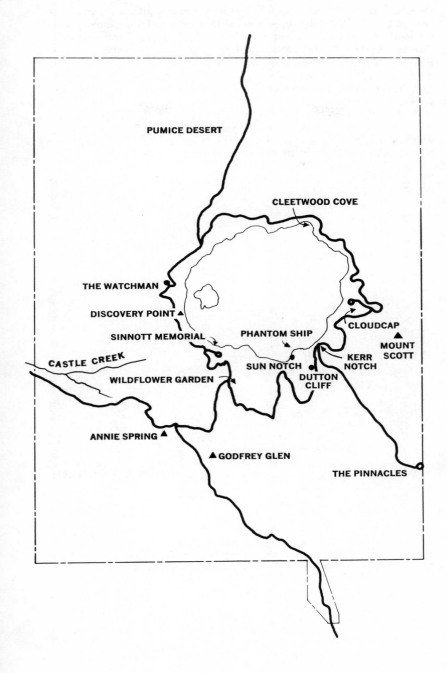

PUMICE DESERT

CLEETWOOD COVE

THE WATCHMAN

DISCOVERY POINT

SINNOTT MEMORIAL

PHANTOM SHIP

CLOUDCAP

MOUNT SCOTT

CASTLE CREEK

SUN NOTCH

KERR NOTCH

WILDFLOWER GARDEN

DUTTON CLIFF

ANNIE SPRING

GODFREY GLEN

THE PINNACLES

the photo story of Crater Lake. From here you can take a six-mile branch road to Lost Creek campground and the *Pinnacles*, spires of pumice and tuff, reminders of ancient fumaroles, rising two hundred feet out of Wheeler Creek Canyon. At *Sun Notch*, a short trail provides another outstanding view of Phantom Ship, which you may want to try early in the day with sunrise spread across the lake. *Garfield Peak*, reached by trail from the lodge at Rim Village, provides climaxing views in all directions from almost nineteen hundred feet above the lake.

Winter affords excellent opportunities for perfect reflections of high peaks in the mirrorlike water and for high snowbanks along the road to the rim, which is kept open by plowing. Likewise, the one-mile section from Rim Village to Discovery Point is usually open throughout the winter.

Crater Lake, the deepest lake in the United States, is cradled in an extinct volcano. The lake is framed with evergreen forests of pine, fir, and hemlock, and you can view the entire lake at once from the rim of lava cliffs.

Everglades National Park
P.O. Box 279
Homestead, Florida 33030

The largest subtropical wilderness in the continental United States presents a spectacular display in winter and early spring of rare, beautiful birdlife in its native habitat. But the sensitive photographer will perceive even more in the biological integrity of the Everglades environment. If you can focus your mind's eye on the life community of a landscape with maximum elevation of ten feet, and search for the living, dynamic character of land, water, vegetation, and wildlife, then you will shoot creative pictures of true impact and distinction.

Seasonal conditions vary considerably and influence photographic activity. Most of southern Florida's rainfall, which averages about sixty inches a year, falls during the summer, when spectacular cloud formations develop. Water levels are high, scattering the wildlife and painting the vegetation lush shades of green. This is the best time to photograph flowers, although many tropical species bloom throughout the year. Summer rains also bring insects, for which visitors should prepare themselves. During winter, water levels drop very low, causing much vegetation to turn yellow and brown and concentrating wildlife around waterholes that become reservoirs of life. Besides the great displays of birds colored blue, green, black, yellow, and red, there are striking tropical insects, giant spiders, and a variety of reptiles—unusual and beautiful animals to be photographed against a background of tropical vegetation, water, and sky.

Everglades National Park lies a little more than an hour by car from Miami through the town of Homestead. The western water gateway at Everglades is the boater's entrance on the Gulf Coast.

Picture-Taking Stops

Approaching from Homestead, the *Visitor Center* near the park entrance should be your first of several stops on the thirty-eight-mile road to Flamingo, the main center of activity. Exhibits will give you the foundation to appreciate the aquatic-based ecosystem. Then, along the park road, six nature trails penetrate different habitats, each supporting specific plants and animals. First is the *Anhinga Trail,* where an elevated boardwalk across the slough features a wildlife show with alligators, water snakes, and a variety of wading birds. Such sloughs, ponds, and solution holes are the deeper places in the Everglades. *Pa-Hay-Okee,* with an elevated platform eight feet above the landscape, provides photographers with a panorama of the sea of sawgrass stretching to the horizon, punctuated by tree "islands." The *Pineland Trail* leads into one of these islands, dominated by a tropical Caribbean pine found only in Florida in its U.S. range. Prehistorically, natural fires maintained the pinelands, burning back the hardwood understory and permitting the fire-resistant pine to propagate. The *Mahogany Hammock Trail* is also of special interest; such hammocks occur on elevations mere inches above the

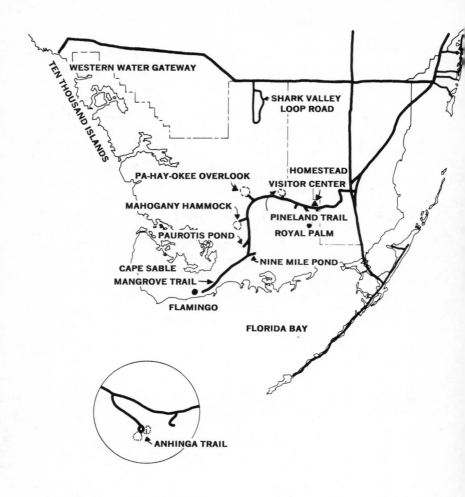

surrounding sawgrass but are characterized by dense hardwood vegetation of West Indian origin. This trail pierces the last virgin stand of West Indian mahogany in the United States, while the area near the turnoff is a favorite roost of immature bald eagles. And the *Mangrove Trail* is part of the belt where the river of sawgrass yields to the coastal brackish and saltwater prairie dominated by mangroves. It is the mixture of clear fresh waters of the glades and saline-rich waters of the mangrove rivers that produces microscopic life, the foundation in the food chain for fish and birds.

Several other turnouts along the road and special favorites of wildlife photographers. *Paurotis Pond* and *Nine Mile Pond* both afford picture possibilities, with their throngs of birds in late winter and early spring. West Lake is black with coots and winter-migrating ducks; eagles are often seen here too. Between West Lake and Flamingo, two roadside ponds are concentration areas for aquatic life and therefore provide excellent opportunities for bird pictures. The best times for this activity are early morning, when the birds feed undisturbed, and late evening, when they return from other areas to roost.

In the *Flamingo* area there are many photographic opportunities. For one thing, you can take pictures of your family at the subtropical tip of the U.S. mainland, where an old fishing village was located before establishment of the park. The *Visitor Center* contains displays and dioramas on Everglades history, from ancient Indian-mound builders to modern crusaders in behalf of rare and endangered bird species. Directly in front of the Visitor Center, shore birds, pelicans, ospreys, and some waders frequent the mud flats. Snake Bight, a shallow cove in Florida Bay accessible by a two-mile trail, is a prime feeding area for shore birds and waders, including the rare reddish egret and several refugee flamingos. The *Bear Lake Trail* offers a fine and varying bird show. The *Christian Point Trail* penetrates a buttonwood forest where migrant birds traverse the coastal prairie and wading birds congregate at low tide. Stark forms of bleached buttonwood snags on the prairie are remnants of the forest that was cut and burned for charcoal near the turn of the century—these snags and the beautiful orchids and airplants they support will reward the skills of any photographer.

The degree to which a photographer—or any visitor—realizes the park's potential depends on the extent to which he takes to footpaths and waterways. Each afternoon about five o'clock, boats depart on a one-hour sunset cruise into Florida Bay, dotted by low-lying islands, or keys. The brilliant red of the setting sun with flocks of birds silhouetted against the sky should produce exceptional color pictures and movies. To take sunset pictures with automatic or nonadjustable cameras, just aim and shoot. With an adjustable camera use a lens opening two stops larger than for a conventional front-lighted scene in sunlight. Much of the backcountry is accessible only by boat. Visitors without their own craft may rent skiffs or houseboats at Flamingo to explore the waterways that interlace the mangrove complex or the open waters of Florida Bay. Visitors may take canoes or boats with 5 1/2-horsepower motors or less down the old *Homestead Canal* to a cluster of lakes inhabited in the winter by throngs of ducks and a good variety of waders, including night herons. The canoe is by all odds the best vehicle for good photography, being quiet, stable, and slow.

Cape Sable, accessible by boat from Flamingo, should certainly be on the itinerary. Along the tropical beach the bounty of seashells is a picture-taker's delight. From June till August giant loggerhead turtles crawl onto the beaches to lay their eggs; this nocturnal sight is not often seen but is worth every effort of the determined photographer. Near Cape Sable, Lake Ingraham supports a marvelous concentration of birds, including white pelicans, during the fall and winter.

In the northern part of the park, the *Shark Valley Loop Road,* a fifteen-mile swing off the Tamiami Trail, cuts deep into the sawgrass and hammock country. Birds concentrate in feeding areas along the road, while alligators gather in numbers in the moat around the forty-foot observation tower at mid-station. Photographers coming down the west coast should not overlook mangrove-wilderness trips conducted by boat from Everglades past shell mounds built by Calusa Indians two thousand years ago. Boat trips are operated in the evening before twilight, to the Ten Thousand Island area.

Glacier National Park
West Glacier, Montana 59936

The great wilderness park of a million acres in the northern Rockies is named for the frozen rivers of ice that sculptured the sharp peaks, the huge rock amphitheaters, and more than two hundred sparkling lakes. Few areas in the western United States have a richer variety and abundance of trees and wildflowers waiting to be enjoyed and photographed. Besides all these, here you can have the experience of hiking or riding up to explore the glaciers themselves.

One of the outstanding scenic motor routes in the world, Going-to-the-Sun Highway, the fifty-mile link between St. Mary Lake on the east side and Lake McDonald on the west, crosses the Continental Divide at Logan Pass, climbing gently while unfolding vistas of lakes, waterfalls, and high cliffs and providing access to walking trails and field trips. Naturalist-conducted walks are held at various points daily. They range from short, easy treks lasting less than two hours to strenuous hikes of two days. Guided pack trips, with time for fishing, hiking, and photography, can be arranged with the park-approved outfitter. If you're concerned about the possible hazard of grizzly bears, it's a good idea to stick with a naturalist or outfitter's guide in the wilderness. Glacier has a tremendous treasure of animals to see and photograph, which are harmless at a distance but may be dangerous when approached or startled. Use telephoto lens if you have one, and keep a respectable distance—even lovable, tame-acting deer might strike without warning with their razor-sharp hooves.

Picture-Taking Stops

You can plan an interesting sequence of pictures or movies on the Going-to-the-Sun Highway. Starting from the west side, *Lake McDonald*, a perfect example of a glacial lake, is the largest lake in the park. An early-morning walk along the lakeshore should provide the chance to shoot waterbirds and shorebirds, including the Grinnell water thrush, a rare warbler, teetering its tail while walking along the water's edge. The tree with fernlike leaves common in the valley is western red cedar, often forming a somber forest with hemlock, larch, and white pine. A few miles beyond, *Avalanche Creek* is the start of a twenty-minute self-guiding trail, with numerous plants identified along the stream-cut gorge. You may be able to photograph a water ouzel, an unusual little bird, bobbing in and out of the water in search of insects. This part of the highway is a good place for wildlife. Moose may appear on the valley floor above the lake, and elk sometimes above Avalanche. Mountain goats are seen on cliffs on either side of the road, usually early or late in the season, or on cool days. The best times are early morning and late afternoon and evening. Black bears are a virtual nuisance, but not to be underestimated. Take pictures of them only from a safe distance.

About twenty miles past the foot of Lake McDonald, the road tunnels through a shoulder of limestone. Two windows have been cut in the tunnel, the upper one framing massive, snow-capped Heavens Peak effectively for

You can photograph the sunrise from atop Cadillac Mountain. Sunrises and sunsets are easy to record because exposure isn't critical.

Sandy beaches make good backgrounds for title pictures. Include some titles among your travel pictures to help tell the story of your trip.

Through a close-up picture, you can capture and record the delicate beauty of wild flowers such as this tiny Solomon's seal.

You will see fascinating views of marine life in Acadia Park. Move in for close-ups of tiny sea creatures such as these starfish.

Left. A footpath leads along a rocky ledge to this boxlike gorge which was carved through limestone by the Rio Grande River. Photograph the vast Big Bend frontier from its many hiking trails.

Top right. The Rio Grande River offers a scenic trip for expert boatsmen. The river is at its best from November to February. Be sure to photograph all the aspects of your picturesque voyage.

Center right. The Big Bend frontier spreads out into a vast adventureland, waiting to be photographed from a multitude of viewpoints along the hiking trails.

Lower right. One of the many stops during the daylong horseback trip to the South Rim in Big Bend. Always be sure to hold your camera level so the horizon line will be level in your pictures.

BRYCE CANYON

Along the main trail in Bryce Canyon, you can photograph the many unusual rock formations. For color slides, use KODACHROME II, KODACHROME-X, KODAK EKTACHROME-X, or KODAK High Speed EKTACHROME Film. For color prints, use KODACOLOR-X Film.

A geological story unfolds in the Canyonlands where you'll see a tableau of multicolored masses of stone in many natural architectural formations. To record the delicate coloring of these rock formations, photograph them with side-lighting or back-lighting.

The towering spires and arches will dazzle your imagination. Back-lighting created a silhouette of these rocks.

You can take jeep tours conducted by local guides, hike, or ride a horse into the heart of the Canyonlands.

CARLSBAD CAVERNS

Carlsbad Caverns provides tours which allow ample time for you to take pictures of the mineral formations which are beautifully illuminated with colored lights. Exposure information is given to those taking the special photo tours.

Although the lighting in Carlsbad Caverns isn't bright enough for you to take hand-held pictures, you can make time exposures. Put your camera on a firm support such as a tripod whenever you use a shutter speed longer than 1/30 second. This picture was exposed for 8 seconds at f/8 on KODAK High Speed EKTACHROME Film, Type B.

CRATER LAKE

Although you may not be able to take an aerial picture like this view of Crater Lake, there are many beautiful areas around the lake that you will be able to photograph. Make sure you take along a good supply of film.

The Everglades abounds with interesting wildlife subjects, such as the snowy egret. If you visit the park, it may be possible to capture the bird's natural grace in a picture you'll be proud to have in your collection.

GLACIER

Glaciers carved the many lakes which dot the Glacier Park wilderness. You can hike on the foot trails, or explore the park on horseback over the many riding trails that will take you deep into the heart of this rugged, but beautiful, unspoiled country.

GRAND CANYON

Top left. From Hopi Point on the South Rim of the Grand Canyon, you can photograph this view of The Battleship. Long shadows create contrast and show the texture of the rocks which adds interest to the picture.

Top right. On the North Rim at Bright Angel, you can photograph another spectacular view. Early and late in the day, the shadows are deep and the colors intense. At midday the colors are more pastel.

It is often difficult to recreate the vastness of the Canyon in photographs without including something of familiar size for comparison. Including people in the foreground of some of your pictures is an easy way to provide the comparison.

A weather-beaten fence makes a picturesque foreground for this log cabin in Jackson Hole, which is at the base of the Grand Tetons. Whenever you compose a picture, look at your subject from several different viewpoints, then shoot from the angle that looks the best.

The Chapel of the Transfiguration in Jackson Hole is framed by the entrance gate. Unusual viewpoints and frames help emphasize the main subject.

The person and weather-beaten tree in the foreground add depth to the picture and direct the viewer's attention toward the Grand Tetons.

Cool, clear mountain streams race down the slopes of the Great Smoky Mountains. The figure in this picture adds a center of interest and a spot of color. To insure the sharpest pictures, hold the camera rock-steady and gently squeeze the shutter release.

The water from this fast-running mountain stream cascades over solid rock to create Laurel Falls. The person provides a good comparison for the size of the falls, and the red jacket provides a contrast of color against the light water and dark rocks.

This 5-foot Haleakala silversword grows naturally only on the slopes of Haleakala Volcano on the Island of Maui. The purplish-brown blossoms and silvery-green leaves of this plant make it an interesting subject for pictures.

Devastation Trail is a wooden boardwalk laid across black pumice, or volcanic ash, which falls from an erupting volcano. The ash strips the foliage from the trees and kills them, leaving this eerie scene. Be sure to photograph your friends and family in all the parks you visit.

From vantage points high along the trail through Isle Royale, you can photograph the fjordlike harbors and surrounding islets. The photographer used a nearby tree to frame this scene and fill in an otherwise blank and uninteresting sky.

The Joshua trees stand at attention along the road into Kings Canyon. For bright, snappy pictures, make sure the camera lens is clean. When necessary, wipe the lens with a clean, soft cloth, such as a handkerchief.

Interesting foreground can turn an ordinary scene into an exciting, colorful picture. Wild flowers add a dash of color to this picture.

From high in the hills, comes this breath-taking view of the Kings River flowing down Kings River Canyon at the foot of Mt. Baxter.

Lassen is a dormant volcano which had its last series of eruptions in the spring of 1914. However, it is still emitting heat and gases, and you can photograph the thermal features such as bubbling hot springs. Back-lighting or side-lighting will help emphasize the steam in your pictures.

photography. Parking space is available on either side of the tunnel. The view of the peaks of the Livingstone Range on the west is increasingly better as you climb higher. The stunted, wind-beaten trees growing in thick clumps along the way are alpine fir; along with wildflowers, you may want to keep a photo record of trees, identifying them by elevation, weather, and soil association.

The *Logan Pass Visitor Center,* astride the Continental Divide, is not only the climax of the motor tour but also the start of walking trips to record and long remember. The choicest is the overnight hike to Granite Park Chalets, following the face of the rugged Garden Wall. Even the least robust photographer should follow the self-guiding *Hidden Lake Overlook Trail,* a two-mile route through a luxuriant alpine meadow carpeted with wildflowers and snow patches. These trips offer chances to photograph the beautiful white-tailed ptarmigan (the bird of high places), gray-crowned rosy finch, marmot, ground squirrel, Rocky Mountain pika, possibly a mountain goat.

Continuing down the east side past towering upswept peaks, the road enters a different kind of forest, composed of alpine fir, spruce, and lodgepole pine. You can use these trees as the foreground to frame pictures of Mt. Jackson and Gunsight Mountain. In the *Sun Point* area, the Water Ouzel Trail offers another good chance for pictures on the mile-long walk to lovely Baring Falls. Then you will want to shoot bow-shaped *St. Mary Lake* from various angles. One of the best is from the bend in the road called the Narrows: with wide-angle lens, shoot with trees in the foreground of the majestic blue lake, cradled in soaring peaks, with the snowfields of Gunsight and Fusillade giving depth to the scene. Another classic view is from the foot of the lake, with peaks from Curly Bear to Gunsight rising above the lake and bordering forest. Finally, you can show your family at the *St. Mary Visitor Center* to conclude the Going-to-the-Sun Highway sequence (or use it as the opener, after the entrance sign, if you're traveling from east to west).

Try to supplement your story with a good trail trip—after all, Glacier has one thousand miles of trail and is noted as a hiker's park. Choose one to match your stamina and time available, bearing in mind that the more time you spend, the more unusual your pictures will be. If you go to Sperry or Granite Chalets, you'll get pictures of clouds swirling around the gabled rooftops of the country. One of the most photogenic objectives is the prominent *Grinnell Glacier,* reached on a daily conducted hike. The slopes of Grinnell Mountain are places to see mountain goats, and sometimes grizzly bear and mountain sheep. Acres upon acres of the slopes are covered with creamy-white flowered beargrass, the park flower. You'll get good shots of the naturalist leading the way over the glacier, probing ahead with an ice ax for soft spots in the tricky snow. Stay alert and follow his instructions while taking pictures of deep crevasses and caves of blue-white ice. Another good trip leads from Many Glacier Valley through fields of wildflowers to Iceberg Lake, in a high glacial cirque, where chunks of snowbank slip into the lake and float like bergs.

For another perspective, excursion launches are operated on several of the park's lakes. One of the best starts from *Many Glacier Hotel* (a worthy picture in itself, a showpiece of another era) on Swiftcurrent Lake. Special cruises are scheduled for photographers only, usually in early morning, with plenty of time to shoot the surroundings of the Garden Wall, Grinnell Glacier, Swiftcurrent Mountain, Mount Wilbur, and the Pinnacle Wall.

No trip to Glacier is complete without a drive north across the Canadian border to *Waterton Lake National Park,* the companion piece in forming the

International Peace Park. This is reached via Chief Mountain International Road, on the eastern flank of the park, from which you can photograph monolith-like *Chief Mountain*. From the Canadian side, a highly scenic launch trip runs across the international boundary to the modernistic *Waterton Visitor Center*, interpreting the cooperation by two nations in preserving this sanctuary of nature.

Most visitors come to Glacier during the summer. June has special appeal, with a wealth of flowers. September is interesting too, with scarlet autumn berries and yellow and orange leaves adding color to the tableau.

In Glacier National Park, more than a million acres of wilderness and sparkling lakes are waiting for you. You can take the scenic motor route through the park, take a guided pack trip which allows time for fishing and picture-taking, or explore the many hiking trails.

Grand Canyon National Park
Grand Canyon, Arizona 86023

One of America's gifts to the world is the protection of this special place of natural beauty and unlimited scientific values. In form, size, and glowing color, nothing approaches the Grand Canyon. The gigantic chasm has sometimes been called the greatest of the seven wonders and has been photographed from every conceivable angle. Still it waits for one more picture to reflect a new mood and new meaning.

The abyss is one mile deep and four to fourteen miles wide. The second-longest river in the United States, the Colorado, rushes to the sea through the canyon bottom. Whole ranges of mountains rise from the depths, their tops only slightly below the rim of the gorge, which slashes a wilderness plateau for over two hundred miles. The whole spectacle reveals the story of erosion, the unending change in the earth's crust.

Picture-Taking Stops

The South Rim, the main center of activity, is developed along a thirty-five-mile section; pictures can easily be taken from every mile at every hour. It is sometimes said that midday should be avoided because the sun is nearly vertical, precluding side-lighting and back-lighting, but try it for yourself—you may find the canyon painted in memorable searing reds.

The photographer's day properly should begin before the sun rises, setting up equipment (preferably including tripod) and enjoying the richness of the area. Sunrise can be photographed from nearly any point, but try *Desert View* or *Lipan Point* near the end of the East Rim Drive. Once the sun comes up, from this vantage you can get a variety of scenes, of huge rock formations etched by cool morning shadows, the winding Colorado River far below, the Painted Desert stretching eastward, and the Watchtower perched on a high rocky point. You can climb the tower, built of native stone, and shoot panoramas far into the surrounding Indian country. Use the tower itself as part of the Indian story, for it contains a reproduction of a ceremonial kiva, Indian pictographs, and symbolic paintings by the noted Hopi artist Fred Kabotie.

From here you can stop at the *Tusayan Ruins* and museum, a small prehistoric pueblo with displays tracing early human history of the canyon. Then work your way back toward Grand Canyon Village and the West Rim, stopping along the way to shoot for new angles into the yawning depths from *Moran Point, Grandview Point,* and *Yaki Point;* with telephoto lens you can follow hikers on the Kaibab Trail winding steeply into the canyon. From *Mather Point,* the most popular spot on the South Rim, you can shoot wide panoramas, as well as follow Bright Angel Creek flowing through the great gash of Bright Angel Canyon. You'll get a lot of background and visual orientation at the *Yavapai Museum,* where the naturalist explains the story of two billion years of history recorded in the rock walls. The museum makes a great photo itself, with the naturalist pointing to the relief model and the Grand Canyon framed by the picture window behind him.

Continuing eastward, follow the *Canyon Rim Nature Trail*, which affords views from unfenced and undeveloped vantages. You can trace hikers or mule riders down Bright Angel Trail, a route pioneered by prehistoric Indians and improved by prospectors who ran it as a toll trail. Far down below you'll spot the trail passing through Indian Gardens, and the noted landmark formation called the Battleship above it. Use the plant life along the rim, including cholla cactus, leaf yucca, gnarled Utah juniper, sagebrush, piñon, and ponderosa pine, as subjects in themselves, as well as for foreground and framing.

Canyon Village, the year-round center, provides many picture opportunities, even including the hotels. El Tovar and Bright Angel Lodge have stood for more than half a century, native stone and log silhouetted against the rim, with subjects of interest inside and out. *Hopi House* is patterned after the ancient Hopi pueblos, with log beams protruding from the walls to support upper stories and roofs. Each afternoon a group of Hopi Indian dancers performs on the stone platform, a suggestion of the true ancient ceremonial which is reserved for the native people within the reservation.

West Rim Drive covers eight miles, passing excellent photo points, including the head of Bright Angel Trail and *Hopi Point*. This is a special place at sunset and even after, when the lingering alpenglow bathes the canyon—a good time for a short time exposure with your camera on a tripod. The Inner Gorge, the narrow, V-shaped slot running through the bottom of the canyon, is a mighty canyon by itself, through which the turbulent Colorado River carves its way with silt, sand, and boulders. Other stops along the West Rim, particularly at *Mohave Point* and *Pima Point*, will provide different angles and open vistas of the spectacular Monument Creek basin. *Hermit's Rest*, at the end of the Rim Drive, is furnished as it was more than half a century ago—a good interior setting.

Transportation has changed many things, but the best (and only) ways into the canyon are by foot and muleback. It takes a good hiker to make it all the way to the floor and back, or across to the North Rim, but there's a shorter trip to *Cedar Ridge* full of picture potential; anyone in good health can make it on a mule for the one-or two-day trips. The longer trip goes to the very bottom. Start by shooting the action around the red barn and corral, then get your fellow riders on the switchbacks of Jacob's Ladder cut into sheer cliffs between Grandeur and Maricopa points. Keep the camera strap around your neck or wrist, and don't worry about your safety—the sure-footed mule wants to get back in one piece too. You'll stop for lunch, and pictures, at the cottonwood oasis of *Indian Gardens*, then continue down the zigzag course to the roaring river, between sheer walls only three hundred feet apart, where you should allow enough exposure for shadowy spots. The famous *Kaibab Suspension Bridge*, just wide enough for a pack mule, will be a photo highlight on the canyon floor before reaching the oasis of *Phantom Ranch*, the small guest ranch alongside Bright Angel Creek, restored after being partly damaged in the flood of 1967. Next morning you return by the Kaibab Trail, equally colorful but a little shorter. You can continue up the Kaibab Trail, crossing and recrossing Bright Angel Creek and stopping for pictures at aptly named *Ribbon Falls* before reaching the North Rim.

The *North Rim* offers an entirely different photographic kaleidoscope. Being higher and cooler, it bears the mantle of a Canadian spruce forest rather than an Arizona desert. Look for the chance to photograph the white-tailed, black-bodied Kaibab squirrel, which is unknown on the South Rim. The tip of the promontory, *Bright Angel Point*, juts a mile into the canyon, flanked by Roaring Springs Canyon and the Transept, with spectacular vistas in all directions, even including the Grand Canyon Lodge, perched on the rim behind. Cape Royal Drive leads twenty-six miles across the Walhalla Plateau to important photo points at *Angel's Window* and *Cape Royal.* From *Point Imperial,* the highest point of the entire rim, you can shoot across Painted Desert, Marble Canyon, and the Little Colorado River where it joins the main stream. A less-developed road leads from the park entrance across the forest of pine, spruce, and aspen to *Point Sublime,* the closest point along the rim to the Inner Gorge, and views of spectacular buttes and temples. Pictures at dusk can give a misty Oriental feeling to these scenes.

For even more detailed information, you may want to obtain a copy of the booklet "How to Photograph the Grand Canyon," which is sold in the park. The serious photographer who wants to do a complete picture story of the Grand Canyon should not overlook the efficient and accommodating sightseeing charter-airplane service operating from the airport on the South Rim. He can do many other things as well, given ambition, time, and patience, such as visiting Toroweap Point in the remote Grand Canyon National Monument for a vertical shot three thousand feet down sheer rock walls; and running the river in a rubber raft, an increasingly popular form of wilderness recreation, tracing the course of the mighty Colorado from its junction with the Green River in Canyonlands National Park, through Glen Canyon National Recreation Area, Grand Canyon National Park, and adjoining National Monument, into Lake Mead National Recreation Area.

It's often called the seventh wonder of the world because the abyss of the Grand Canyon offers an extravaganza of natural beauty and color. Whole ranges of mountains rise from the depths of the canyon, and the Colorado River rushes along its bottom.

Grand Teton National Park
Moose, Wyoming 83012

The Tetons are among the most photographed mountains in the world, a jagged range of huge peaks forty miles long thrusting skyward above the level plain of Jackson Hole. The canyons and lower slopes are marked by waterfalls and wildflowers and the valley of the Snake River by forest-bordered glacial lakes and streams abounding in fish and waterfowl.

The Tetons are a great block of the earth's crust, heaved up along a fault, or crack, then worn down by erosion and glaciation. Snowfields and small glaciers hanging in the peaks, typical U-shaped canyons and cirques at the heads, and terminal moraines rimming the lakes recall the sculpturing forces of the Ice Age. The national park, which covers 310,350 acres, is a few miles north of Jackson and is almost adjacent to Yellowstone.

Picture-Taking Stops

Approaching from the south on the Jackson Hole Highway, the *National Elk Refuge,* immediately adjoining the park, is maintained primarily for winter care of the Jackson Hole elk herd, but you can count on getting pictures of some animals here at any time. These are the first of many forms of Western wildlife you will have a chance to photograph in this living sanctuary. It will help to use a telephoto lens and to keep a considerable distance, for your own safety's sake. Moose can be seen in the early morning and at dusk browsing along river bottoms and fragrant meadows. The sleek pronghorn sometimes appears in small bands on Antelope Flats during summer. Bison are maintained in the wildlife range between Jackson Lake Lodge and the east entrance station; this is where white pelicans often stop on their migrations in spring and fall. One of the prizes of the wildlife photographer is the shy and rare trumpeter swan, sometimes seen in the Elk Refuge and other times on Christian Pond east of Jackson Lake Lodge.

Menor's Ferry is a reconstruction of the pioneer ferry that operated across the Snake River in 1892, following the raw days in Jackson Hole of traders, trappers, and desperadoes. When water level permits, you can photograph a naturalist conducting a demonstration ride. The little wooden *Chapel of the Transfiguration,* nearby, is another jewel of the past; you can shoot the majestic Tetons through the large window behind the altar, a classic frame. The *Moose Visitor Center* contains outstanding dioramas on the early mountain men and fur traders who followed in the pathways of the intrepid John Colter.

Turning north, the Teton Park Road leads to *Jenny Lake,* which makes an excellent picture at the foot of the Cathedral group of the Tetons, especially in early morning, when the blue waters are likely to be calm. You may feel that these mountains need the compositional help of a colorful foreground object; if you use people, ask them to direct attention to the mountains by looking toward them. Jenny Lake is the site of the Exum School of Mountaineering, one of the finest in the country, where you may want to start your teen-ager upward in the world and take pictures of him on the way in one of the major activities of the Tetons. If that's too strenuous, the Park Service maintains nearly two hundred miles of hiking trail, and several of the best opportunities start from or near Jenny Lake. Good hikers will have the chance to photograph mountain flora, patterns of banded gneiss, hanging canyons, craggy passes, lake-filled glacial basins, and glaciers from eye level.

Jackson Lake Lodge is one of the focal points of park activity, providing an interesting photo perspective of the lake and mountains through its huge picture windows. Using flash and color film you can get shots of fine paintings and Indian craft pieces in the lobby and public rooms. Sometimes you may see moose feeding in the marshy areas near the beaver ponds west of the lodge. You can get pictures of your children on horseback rides, from Jackson Lake, or from the Colter Bay development, but there are a variety of other types of rides and pack trips full of possibilities. If you see the film "Trail Ride in the Wilderness," shown every Saturday night at the lodge, you'll get some idea of what you can do on a horse in high country.

From Jackson Lake and Colter Bay, wilderness vistas are close, beginning where the road ends. The trails around *Emma Matilda* and *Two Ocean Lakes* will enable you to shoot beaver lodges, trumpeter-swan nests, and typical habitat of moose, bear, and coyote, if not the subjects themselves. During July and August the open meadows turn bright with paintbrush, balsamroot, scarlet gilia, and lupine.

The *float trip on the Snake River* is not to be missed by the photographer. In the course of following the thirty-mile water trail aboard a rubber raft, you will perhaps photograph an eagle feeding its young in a high nest, beaver at work (or at least the works of beaver), coyote, elk, ducks, heron, and assorted other members of the wild river environment.

The best months to photograph flowers are June and July in Jackson Hole, July and August in the high country. In autumn, when golden aspen glitter on the hillsides, elk are most easily observed and exciting to photograph, with mature bulls rounding up their harems and rivals battling with clashing antlers. In winter, skiing takes over on the slopes of adjoining Teton National Forest. Exceptional pictures can be taken from the chairlifts, with panoramic views encompassing hundreds of miles, and the mighty Tetons dominating the landscape.

Great Smoky Mountains National Park
Gatlinburg, Tennessee 37738

Clear, invigorating air, sparkling streams, and virgin woodlands provide the surroundings for photography in this half-million-acre mountain wilderness. Sunshine, however, is a transient thing. Wispy, low-hanging clouds often roll through the gaps, providing an interesting background. One doesn't complain about the weather in the Smokies; he makes the most of it, as nature does in nurturing forest giants, spring wildflowers, blooming summer plants.

The Smokies lie about an hour's drive from Knoxville, Tennessee, and from Asheville, North Carolina, and within a day's driving time of most large cities of the East and Middle West. But there are reaches of the high places which, in the true spirit of the national parks, invite the photographer afoot to enjoy the unspoiled, unexploited beauty of Appalachia.

Picture-Taking Stops

Starting on the Tennessee side at the *Sugarlands Visitor Center,* Route 441 leads across the mountains through the heart of the Smokies, with scenic turnoffs and self-guiding trails. You'll see plenty of bears; some will chew on anything within reach, including a photographer's arm or leg, so keep your distance and avoid feeding the bears. Stop to take a picture of the Chimney Tops, the twin craggy pinnacles of rock high atop the mountain slope. If you walk into the woods at the foot of the mountain you will join the old *Indian Gap Trail,* which until recent times was the only traversable route between the North Carolina and Tennessee sides of the Smokies. Though weed-grown and shadowy, traces of the trail remain for an interesting mood picture.

From the Chimney campground, the *Big Locust Nature Trail* is unbeatable for spring-wildflower photographers. It passes through an area where settlers once cut the trees, piled the rocks, and cultivated the land; then it plunges into a fragment of virgin forest, including the rare yellowwood, giant tulip tree, black locust, and buckeye. The variety of plant life along this one little trail is incredible—the gray-barked white ash that was growing here above a rock-strewn stream long before the white man arrived; large old sugar maples; young silverbell; basswood; the evergreen walking fern, or "sore-eye," a strange, ancient plant growing on moist mossy rocks, spawning when the tips of its finely tapered fronds touch the ground; and the wildflowers that reach their greatest variety in April. Exercise patience and shoot for the unusual, like the Indian-pipe, a little whitish plant lacking in chlorophyll which appears like a ghost with nodding, bowed head and is known as "corpse plant" or "ghost flower." Remember that side-lighting emphasizes a flower's shape and brings out texture of the petals; back-lighting accentuates the translucent, delicate quality of the flower and creates really striking pictures. Have a reflector, such as aluminum foil stretched over a sheet of cardboard, to bounce light into shadow areas. With a strong close-up lens or two close-up lenses used together, you can focus on the center of a flower and interpret many of nature's own intricate designs.

Another choice trail from the transmountain road leads up through a tun-

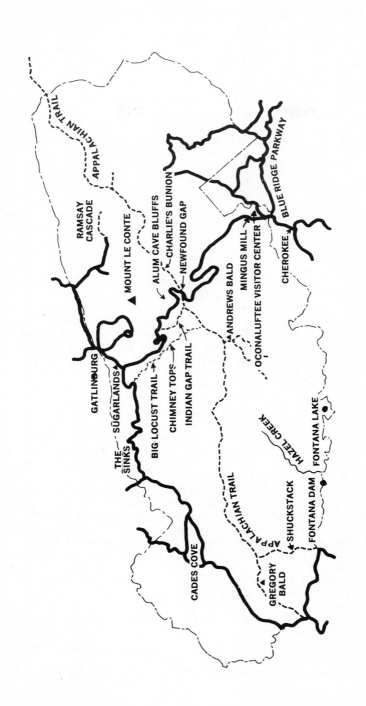

APPALACHIAN TRAIL

RAMSAY CASCADE

▲ MOUNT LE CONTE

ALUM CAVE BLUFFS

CHARLIE'S BUNION

NEWFOUND GAP

BLUE RIDGE PARKWAY

MINGUS MILL

OCONALUFTEE VISITOR CENTER

CHEROKEE

ANDREWS BALD

GATLINBURG

THE SINKS

SUGARLANDS

BIG LOCUST TRAIL

CHIMNEY TOPS

INDIAN GAP TRAIL

HAZEL CREEK

FONTANA LAKE

APPALACHIAN TRAIL

SHUCKSTACK

FONTANA DAM

CADES COVE

▲ GREGORY BALD

nel of rhododendron, passing the immense Arch Rock and a large heath bald, to *Alum Cave,* a massive overhanging cliff of black slate which is one of the landmarks of the park. You can illustrate its dimensions by including other hikers in the picture below the overhang. The "balds" are unique features of the Smokies, mountain meadows of unknown origin outlining peaks and ridges, with vegetation consisting of catawba rhododendron and mountain laurel.

If you continue hiking upward on this route, your reward will be arrival at the summit of *Mount LeConte.* In mid-June rose-purple rhododendron will be spectacular subjects along the way. The round trip can be made in one full day, but it's best to stay over at the famous (but simple) LeConte Lodge. From Cliff Top you can photograph the glorious sunset over hundreds of square miles of mountains, lowlands, East Tennessee towns, and the western horizon darkening through the colors of red, orange, and bluish-white. At daybreak *Myrtle Point* offers another fine vista to be shared with high-flying juncos, warblers, and vireos.

From the *Newfound Gap* overlook, you can get excellent panoramic views of the peaks rising above six thousand feet and extending like green waves to the distant Blue Ridge horizon. Take a picture of your family admiring the bronze plaque to John D. Rockefeller, Jr., benefactor of the park, at the crescent-shaped masonry wall straddling the boundary line between Tennessee and North Carolina. From here you can sample the *Appalachian Trail,* the longest footpath in the world, which follows the crest of the mountains for seventy miles, the full length of the park. You can try it for an hour or all week and never run out of photo subjects. Hiking to the east, in one day you can make it past the Appalachian Trail shelter at Ice Water Spring to *Charlie's Bunion,* an out-crop of bare rock on the jagged ridge of the Sawteeth, offering an excellent vista of silent ridges and wild forest. To the west the trail will take you across Mount Collins and Clingman's Dome, the highest point within the park, and Andrews Bald, covered with high mountain grass, bordered with spruce, rhododendron, and azalea which present a display of flaming color in late June. A small "hanging bog," with mosses and wetland plants, is a special botanical feature.

Descending on Route 441 along the Oconaluftee River on the North Carolina side, *Mingus Mill* presents a water-powered, turbine-driven grist mill as a page out of the past. Likewise, the *Oconaluftee Pioneer Farmstead* provides an excellent opportunity to photograph historic structures and living demonstrations of weaving, muzzle-loading, and shake-splitting, the old crafts of the highlands. On leaving the park, you'll be in the *Cherokee Indian Reservation,* where you can photograph more craftsmen at work at the authentic *Oconaluftee Indian Village* and Qualla Crafts Shop. They serve as a fitting prelude to the evening performance of the outdoor drama "Unto These Hills."

Scenic loop roads virtually encircle and give additional access to the national park. From Cherokee you can drive to Bryson City and then to *Fontana Dam* and *Fontana Lake,* with plenty of boating-and-fishing-picture possibilities. One of the finest experiences for the fisherman-photographer is to rent a boat at Fontana Village and cross to *Hazel Creek,* noted among trout fishermen everywhere. The hiker-photographer should head from the dam to *Shuckstack Fire Tower,* overlooking outstanding panoramas, and from there to Gregory Bald, especially in late June, when spectacular masses of wild azaleas bloom along the edges of the hillside meadow.

Reentering the park via Townsend on the Tennessee side, Cades Cove is a choice subject. White-tail deer are often seen, and occasionally wild turkey, a wildlife photographer's prize. There are many pictures to be taken on the loop road passing open fields, frame churches, the half-dozen working farms with their smokehouses and "bee gums," and the overshot waterwheel grist mill. Then, driving back toward Gatlinburg on Route 73, the *Sinks* is a small but especially lovely cascade. The road parallels the winding Little River, fast-flowing and clear, typical of the charming Smoky Mountain streams. And east of Gatlinburg you can walk from Greenbrier Cove through virgin forests of towering hemlock, yellow poplar, black cherry, and white ash, along streams shaded with rhododendron, to *Ramsay Cascade,* a beautiful waterfall high in the hills.

Nature photographers can expect to catch unusual pictures in any season in the Great Smokies. Wildflowers are usually outstanding for the Spring Wildflower Pilgrimage, held annually at Gatlinburg the last weekend in April, with botany lectures, photography seminar, and bird walks. In autumn the beauty of the hardwood forests changing color is one of the high spots of Appalachia.

Great Smoky Mountains National Park offers a half million acres of mountain wilderness with clear mountain streams flowing through its woodlands. The Big Locust Nature Trail is popular for its outstanding display of wild flowers in the spring.

Haleakala National Park
P.O. Box 456
Kahului, Maui, Hawaii 96732

On the fair island of Maui, formed by volcanic eruptions on the ocean's floor millions of years ago, the ancient Haleakala crater reminds visitors of the power of the earth's forces. Richly colored cinder deposits, cones, and lava flows characterize the landscape and await the photographer, along with beautiful native plants and rare birds, including the Hawaiian goose, or nene.

Haleakala, a great volcano, thirty-three miles long and 10,023 feet high, is deeply woven into native Polynesian legend and mythology. The park covers 26,403 acres on the "Valley Isle," the second largest in the Hawaiian group. The island is less than forty minutes by plane from Honolulu over a seventy-mile stretch of water. The most favorable weather for picture-taking is in summer, especially in very early morning or afternoon, in contrast to midday, which is often foggy. Late afternoon in particular presents the greatest range of colors for photographing the crater from the rim. Photographers should bring plenty of film, since none is sold in the park; they should also understand that the nearest food and gasoline are twelve miles from the entrance.

Picture-Taking Stops

Approaching from Kahului, the island's center of population, about thirty miles away, the crater comes clearly into sight. The road climbs through plantations and ranchlands to the park entrance and *Hosmer Grove* and picnic area, the best place to photograph native birds. These include the golden plover (the noted Alaska-Hawaii commuter), the bright scarlet iiwi, scarlet apapane, and amakihi. Native high-altitude plants like sandalwood and silver geranium create an interesting tableau, mingling with transplanted species like juniper and Colter pine.

Halemauu Trail leads one mile from the main park road to the crater rim. You can get excellent views of the trail dropping eighteen hundred feet to the crater floor with a series of switchbacks. On a clear day the view to the left encompasses the blue Pacific and deep green of the lush Koolau rain forest. The view to the right faces cinder cones and lava flows. *Leleiwi Overlook* provides a good view of distant switchbacks on the trail. In late afternoon the shadow cast on the clouds comes from the Specter of the Brocken at the end of the crater. *Kalahaku Overlook* furnishes a stark and scenic view of cinder cones within the crater. This area contains an enclosure of the silversword plant, which is almost as well known as the crater itself. Before blooming, the plant grows as a rounded mass of stiletto-shaped leaves, producing purplish blooms. The silversword and other native plants were nearly exterminated by souvenir hunters, but they are now slowly recovering. The *Visitor Center* contains exhibits and models that help the photographer understand the park story and how the Hawaiian Islands, thousands of miles from any continent, support a complex system of plants and animals through evolutionary change. Sunrise and late-afternoon light both bring out the best colors of the crater formations from this point.

Red Hill Overlook Building, located on the highest point of the rim (as well as the island), also affords excellent sunset photographs. On a clear day exceptional views can be obtained down the outside slope; in fact, the whole "valley" part of the island spreads out ten thousand feet below, and several of the other islands of the chain can be seen.

Over thirty miles of hiking trails offer the photographer an ever-changing view that abounds with picture possibilities. Trails go from steep cliffs to cinder flats, from rough, barren lava flows to lush rain forests, and from native Hawaiian plants and birds to ancient rock structures built by early Hawaiian people. Of special interest is Paliku, a lush oasis deep inside the northeast corner of the crater, where the nene, virtually extinct until its reintroduction here in 1962, feeds upon grasses, leafy plants, and berries. Three cabins are located in the crater and are available to hikers by reservation.

Hawaii Volcanoes National Park
Hawaii 96718

Millions of years ago the floor of the Pacific Ocean trembled and cracked. Lava and hot gases were released, building steadily upward, ultimately creating the chain of Hawaiian Islands. The last and largest, the island of Hawaii, ninety-three miles long and seventy-six miles wide, is almost twice as large as all the other islands combined.

America's greatest volcanic wonderland was set apart by Congress in 1916 as Hawaii National Park; however, Haleakala, on the island of Maui, one of the most colorful volcanoes in the world, became the center of a separate national park in 1961. Mighty Kilauea, the world's most active volcano, and Mauna Loa are the focal points of the national park on Hawaii, the "big island." The epitome of photographic good luck and challenge is to arrive on the scene in the midst of one of their intermittent eruptions (the 1949 eruption continued for almost five months, and there have been others, of shorter duration, since), for Hawaii is perhaps the only place on earth where spectators rush *toward* the volcanic action instead of away from it. These gentle giants seldom become dangerous even while gushing molten lava mixed with sulfurous steam.

If you are fortunate enough to arrive during an eruption, be sure you have high-speed color film and, if possible, a telephoto lens to capture the demonstration of rare natural beauty. Those watching eruptions at night often become concerned about exposure times, since light meters and automatically adjusting cameras do not accurately measure the red glow emitted by cascading lava. Cameras set at 1/15 to 1/30 second and a wide *f*-stop such as *f*/2.8 will capture the gushing "fountains" of lava with KODAK High Speed EKTACHROME Film, Daylight Type.

Picture-Taking Stops

Approaching from Hilo on Route 11, your first stop should be the main *Visitor Center* at park headquarters, where many photographers take pictures of cutaway models, dioramas, and beautiful oil paintings that explain the function of Kilauea Volcano. The large relief map, with all historic lava flows labeled, is worth shooting from different angles. Daily programs include a color movie of recent eruptions.

From the Visitor Center your route should follow the 11.1-mile *Crater Rim Drive*, circling the Kilauea caldera. If you drive southwest (counterclockwise), you'll get fine views across the caldera, starting at the *Kilauea Picnic Ground*. The next point of interest, the *Hawaiian Volcano Observatory*, on the rim of the west wall, also provides an excellent opportunity to view and photograph the caldera; the main crater, Halemaumau, on the caldera floor, can be photographed as a complete subject.

On reaching *Halemaumau Overlook*, the visitor can, by looking all the way around him, tell how the road has dipped to bring him technically inside the volcano itself. Pictures taken of the six-hundred-foot cliffs across Halemaumau will give dramatic illustration. Points of interest are numerous as the road leads back to the rim and into a tree-fern forest, which covers the windward slopes of the volcano. The *Devastation Trail,* a boardwalk across a very fragile pumice-covered area, provides an unequaled opportunity to photograph nature's destruction and spectacular recovery. The cinder cone of Puu Puai, framed with stark branches of dead ohia trees, makes an excellent subject in particular. *Thurston Lava Tube Trail* provides one of the choicest locations for taking pictures of tree ferns and lush tropical plants. Perhaps the final point of interest on Crater Rim Drive is the *Byron Ledge Overlook* at Kilauea Iki crater, scene of the 1959 eruption. From this viewpoint one can look across the crater and view the cinder cone, part of the main caldera, and on a clear day Mauna Loa in the distance.

Many outstanding scenes are found on the park's byroads and hiking trails. The ten-mile *Mauna Loa Strip Road* cuts through lush green flora built on volcanic-ash soil, haunts of brightly colored birds and fantastic lava tree molds, terminating at an altitude of 6,700 feet on the slope of Mauna Loa. The *Hilina Pali Road,* another dead-end drive, winds through acres of waist-high grass, then crosses ancient pahoehoe lava flows, which present weird, grotesque silhouettes to the camera. You can get memorable pictures from the top of Hilina Pali in the late afternoon with the sun setting over the southeast coast and the glistening blue Pacific. Hikers can do even more. The *Mauna Loa Trail* leads to the summit at 13,680 feet, through vast lava fields, winding between pumice cones and along lava-splattered cracks; this trip takes two to three days. The *Halape Coastal Hike,* about eight miles round trip, provides intimate views of a rocky coast and coconut groves meeting the sea.

By car, the *Chain of Craters-Kalapana Road* parallels the ocean for about seven miles, with sea birds, sea arches, thundering surf, and beautiful sunsets serving as colorful picture subjects. This road leads to the *Kaimu Black Sand Beach,* probably the most photographed spot on the island, just outside the southeast entrance to the park.

In general, the area around park headquarters receives about one hundred inches of rain each year. Thus many days are overcast and dark. Fortunately, a rough pattern of daily weather is predictable—most early mornings are clear and bright, but by ten A.M. to noon the trade winds bring a dense cloud cover. The coastal areas are much drier and usually clear. Rain squalls are brief when they do occur, and the clouds can be used to enhance photographs.

Hot Springs National Park
P.O. Box 1219
Hot Springs, Arkansas 71901

The thermal waters in the hills of Arkansas were known and enjoyed by the Indians and the exploring party of Hernando de Soto long before the United States was born. But in 1832, when the government established the springs as a federal reservation, the first step was taken to hold places of special interest in trust for all—which later led to the national-park idea.

Unlike many parks, the season at Hot Springs covers the entire year. Winter temperatures allow for outdoor activities except at infrequent intervals. And while there are year-round photographic attractions, spring and fall offer special features for nature and scenic photography. Although the park is small, covering 1,035 acres, and is nearly surrounded by a busy resort city, the natural values are pleasant and popular. Fifteen miles of hiking trails crisscross the park and offer the best opportunity for its full appreciation.

Picture-Taking Stops

From the *Gulpha Gorge Campground,* set in a beautiful valley two miles from the center of Hot Springs, the photographer can take his choice of several trails. Blooming wildflowers are highlights of the spring, with a continuous display, from the bird's-foot violet and violet wood sorrel in March through the blazing star and butterfly milkweed in May and June. Along both the trails and the *Hot Springs Mountain Scenic Road* flowering dogwood, shadbush, and azalea add color to the shrubs and trees. The 165-foot observation tower provides a broad view of the hilltops and city.

Fall color abounds in October, especially along the *West Mountain Scenic Road* and adjoining trails. Oak, hickory, and other hardwoods provide hardy reds and yellows to mix with the persistent green of the common shortleaf pine, adding life to scenic shots and a colorful background for pictures of your family. You can work with the patterns in the lichens, mosses, ferns, and sedges growing profusely over many interesting rocks, like the fine-grained bluish-white novaculite, dark-green or black mountain shale, and the hard gray Hot Springs sandstone lined with white quartz.

Hydrothermal features of the park, its primary significance, are not so easily available to view. The water is popular for bathing, and the first time most of it reaches the atmosphere is when it pours from a fountain or into a tub at one of the many privately run bathhouses. *Display Springs* are not sealed and still emerge naturally; they are located adjacent to the *Promenade,* a pleasant and relaxing brick-paved walk landscaped in a manner reminiscent of European spas. Jug fountains are located on Reserve Avenue near the park Visitor Center for those wishing to take the hot thermal water home; you can take a picture of one of your family sampling the celebrated elixir.

Isle Royale National Park
Houghton, Michigan 49931

The largest island in Lake Superior is a special place, even among national parks. The only way to reach it is by boat or seaplane. It has no roads, even if you could get a car across the water. It is a natural setting of north woods forest and water wilderness, where the visitor has no need for the chronic haste of daily life.

One of its outstanding features is in the multitude of flowering plants typical of rocky shores, forest floor, bogs, swamps, and open meadows. Many birds and animals are common, but not commonly seen, thus testing the photographer's wisdom and patience. The range includes bald eagle, osprey, pileated woodpecker, wolf, moose, muskrat, mink, and beaver.

The national park covers 539,347 acres of land and water. The island itself is forty-five miles long and about nine miles wide, with lodges at both ends and many walking trails in between. Motor-launch trips can be arranged, affording an excellent way to see and photograph Isle Royale, the "royal island."

Picture-Taking Stops

From mid-June through Labor Day the motor ship "Ranger III" departs from Houghton, Michigan, for Isle Royale three times weekly. Start your picture or movie sequence with a shot of this trim National Park Service vessel at the dock before leaving on the seventy-mile voyage. You can also reach the park aboard private vessels from nearby Copper Harbor and from Grand Portage, Minnesota. Aboard "Ranger III" be sure to photograph the raising of the Houghton-Hancock Bridge, then take pictures as you journey through the Portage Lake Ship Canal and across the shipping lanes of Lake Superior, meeting vessels from distant world ports.

The main port on the island, *Rock Harbor,* has been called the largest, best—and least disturbed—natural harbor in the Great Lakes, from which you can take pictures of outlying islands and rocky islets. During the visitor season ranger-naturalists conduct guided walks to attractive localities, allowing ample time for photography; you can also cover the routes on your own. One trail leads to the mellowed and abandoned *Rock Harbor Lighthouse,* built in 1855 to guide boats into the harbor during the early copper-mining days. Another goes to *Monument Rock,* a towering seventy-foot pinnacle carved through the centuries by waves and winter ice, then continues past ancient beaches and a copper-mining site used by prehistoric Indians to *Lookout Louise* for one of the most beautiful views in the park. The hike to *Mount Franklin* leads through a spruce-fir forest over a series of valleys and ridges. Early in the season (before mid-July) you may find the beautiful calypso orchid growing in the dense forest. In June and July the showy bog kalmia, or laurel, forms an intense display throughout the bogs. By all means travel with a good book on wildflowers so you can identify the plants you're photographing—and where and how to look for them. If wildflowers are your interest, don't miss the *Albert Stoll, Jr., Memorial Trail.* Mount Franklin lies astride the *Greenstone Ridge Trail,* which follows the backbone of the island for forty-two miles. A hiker has many pictures awaiting along this route, including glades purpled with iris, evidences of glacial polishing and grooving on exposed rocks, stops at the Isle Royale shelters, and views from the high points, especially *Mount Ishpeming Lookout,* the highest on the island. Even if you don't go all the way, you can get a good sample by continuing from Mount Franklin to *Ojibway Lookout,* with a superb view from the tower of many lakes and, on a clear day, the Canadian mainland standing out fifteen miles north.

One day you may want to rent a boat for another photo perspective. Nearly every inlet, island, and sound has its cluster of weatherbeaten shanties, wharves, and fishhouses, recalling the age when commercial fishing was an important industry. On the shoreline of popular fishing grounds like *Hay Bay, Chippewa Harbor,* and *Long Point* are numerous worn-out boats to serve as interesting foreground in your pictures. There still are a few commercial fishing bases in operation, with good picture possibilities, but a thoughtful photographer will avoid bothering fishermen at their work. The high spot of your journey afloat will be *Lorelei Lane,* a passage between two chains of islands alternating with rocky bluffs and gravel beaches and the great expanse of Lake Superior stretching to the horizon.

Washington Harbor, near the northwest end of the island, has other points of interest. A fine trail leads along Washington Creek to *Windigo Mine,* the ruins of an old copper pit worked until about 1899. Ancient Indian mining pits will turn up at other locations, some of them dating back almost four thousand years. Your chances are good of seeing and photographing moose along streams or browsing on the shores of inland lakes. The *Feldtman Ridge Trail* follows a terrace consisting of Precambrian red sandstone on the high ridge to Siskiwit Bay, one of the beauty spots of Isle Royale.

The travel season to Isle Royale is relatively short, from mid-June to mid-October. Fog is common during June and July, but this is the best period for wildflower photography. Maples, aspens, and yellow birch add the bonus of changing colors early in September.

Lassen Volcanic National Park
Mineral, California 96063

Cones, crags, lava beds, the hissing Bumpass Hell and steaming Sulfur Works recall the violent past of the most recently active volcano in the continental United States, which staged a major fireworks display in 1915 and continued its eruptions until 1921. Lassen Peak, towering above the scene at 10,457 feet, is the remnant of an ancient volcanic bowl, Mount Tehama.

The national park covers 106,934 acres of evergreen forest and fifty wilderness lakes a little more than one hundred miles east of Redding in northern California. It is a year-round park, with winter snow conditions excellent for cross-country skiing and unusual photography of steaming fumaroles and boiling mud pots.

Picture-Taking Stops

Important scenic and volcanic features can be seen and photographed from the thirty-mile Park Road, which half encircles Lassen Peak in the western part of the park, but such stops are best when they serve as introduction to further picture-taking on the trails. More than one hundred and fifty miles of footpaths lead to lakes, streams, waterfalls, thermal areas, and old volcanoes.

After stopping at the Visitor Center, an excellent vantage point lies on the west side of *Manzanita Lake,* with a view of Lassen Peak reflected in the water. Use the firs and pines for framing your pictures; a choice time is late afternoon or early evening with the alpenglow on the snowy peak. The east side of Manzanita Lake below the campground provides another good view for sunsets. So does the picnic area at Reflection Lake, across the Park Road, with willows and alder dipping their roots into the clear waters.

Farther along the Park Road, at the east side of *Chaos Jumbles,* there is a good view of the pinkish Chaos Crags and Jumbles, towering, pluglike masses pushed up through vents. The end of the Chaos Crags Trail gives a good view of Crags Crater and Crag Lake. The *Hot Rock,* about five miles beyond, is another landmark, a large boulder deposited as part of the great mudflow of 1915. When you reach the *Devastated Area,* stripped of all its vegetation by the 1915 volcanic blast, use the uprooted tree a short distance north of the bridge as your foreground; from this point, afternoon light gives the best shading on the peak.

At the base of *Crescent Crater,* reached by trail, a dramatic close-up of Lassen Peak and the upper Devastated Area unfolds. Late-afternoon light is best, while the flower display in late summer makes a good foreground. Another trail leads to the base of the plugs on the south side of Raker Peak, with a sweeping view of the Devastated Area. An even more sweeping view may be had from the top of the plugs; however, the difference is seldom worth the effort except to enthusiastic rock climbers.

After continuing by car, take a picture of your family reading the *Summit Sign,* marking the highest point on the road (8,512 feet). The *Lassen Peak Trail,* starting from the parking area, takes about four hours round trip but is worth the effort for any photographer. The view from the top overlooks the park's prominent craters, blue lakes, and forests and extends as far as Mount Shasta, seventy-five miles northwest.

At *Kings Creek Meadows,* the east end of Upper Meadow affords a good view of Lassen Peak across the meadow with the stream in the foreground; afternoon light is good, particularly in late summer, when back-lighting emphasizes the warm brown colors of the meadow. The 1.3-mile trail to *Kings Creek Falls* shows Lassen's wildflowers, including crimson snowplant, leopard lily, penstemon, and bleeding heart. *Bumpass Hell* parking area is an excellent site for shooting shiny glacial polish on the rocks and the huge isolated glacial erratic, a boulder left perched on a ridgetop when a glacier melted. On the easy *Bumpass Hell Trail,* the best general view of the bubbling hot springs and mud pots—reminiscent of Yellowstone—is from the overlook point. Individual features within the basin will provide many spectacular subjects. Include human figures in some pictures to dramatize the power of natural forces. Follow the trail beyond Bumpass Hell for a view of Crumbaugh Lake.

Beautiful *Emerald Lake* is well worth shooting from several angles; the color is deepest green in late afternoon. *Little Hot Springs Valley,* because of its location in a deep canyon, will be in shadow at dawn and dusk. The best overall viewpoint is the bank of East Sulfur Creek just below the steam-vent area. Varied colorful boiling pools make good photo subjects. About a quarter mile west of Marker 13 there is a good view of *Pilot Pinnacle,* with the steam vent at its base; a telephoto lens will help to compress the perspective and show the relationship between the mountain and steam vents. At Marker 7 there are good views of Brokeoff Mountain, best with telephoto lens, and the cliffs of Diamond Peak. At the dramatic *Sulfur Works,* a self-guiding trail will bring you within close-up range of steam vents and mud pots in the caldera of ancient Mount Tehama. The best view of the entire thermal area is from the *Ridge Lakes Trail;* midsummer flowers make an attractive foreground. Continuing up the trail, the best view of the lakes is from the south side, showing the brightly colored slopes behind them. The *Brokeoff Mountain Trail* is another photo route too good to miss. Alpine forests, meadows, glacial pools, and permanent snowbanks set against the sheer cliffs and broad slopes offer many possibilities. The view of distant Mount Shasta framed by wind-trimmed hemlocks offers a fine opportunity along the trail, while the view of Lassen Peak from the summit is one of the best in the entire park.

Many good picture possibilities lie along the wilderness trails in the eastern section of the park. With Butte Lake campground in the northeast corner as a gateway, good views can be taken of *Butte Lake,* with the seven-hundred-foot-high Cinder Cone, one of the outstanding volcanic features of the park, in the background. When you photograph the *Cinder Cone Trail,* include people in at least one scene to show the size of the cone. The best overall view is from the Emigrant Trail on the west side. When you climb to the top, the multicolored *Painted Dunes* make a beautiful subject; a polarizing filter will remove the glare and reveal the red, gray, yellow-brown, and orange in the heaps of volcanic cinder and ash. Moving south past Snag Lake, an old log cabin at the edge of Cameron Meadow makes an interesting subject. At *Juniper Lake* the best overall view is from the beach at the north end, with Mount Harkness in the background.

Devil's Kitchen Trail, in the southern portion of the park, leads to perhaps the largest and most active hydrothermal areas in the park. Its features include violently steaming fissures and the park's two largest mud pots, excellent subject matter for movies, especially since their activity may change at any time. Use extra caution on this route.

Mammoth Cave National Park
P.O. Box 68
Mammoth Cave, Kentucky 42259

A century ago it was regarded as the greatest cave in the world. It was so renowned that the immortal Jenny Lind came to sing, and Edwin Booth, the Shakespearean actor, to recite Hamlet's soliloquy (in a room now called Booth's Amphitheater). Following its discovery in 1798, visitors had come first by stagecoach, then by steamboat up the Green River, or by rail. Then the crowds came in increasing numbers from all corners of the country.

Even today nobody knows how mammoth the cave in the "Land of Ten Thousand Sinks" really is. It consists of many miles of charted passageways, filled with spectacular rock formations and domes, and uncounted miles still unexplored. The subtle processes of nature, which begin with rainwater seeping into the ground and dissolving layers of limestone, continue to form new caves and to decorate the older ones.

You will need flash to take pictures in the cave. It won't always be easy, and you cannot take good flash pictures of distant subjects with ordinary flash equipment—professionals use multiple flash, as many as thirty units in the large rooms. Even with single flash you can still get some interesting photos, vignettes, and profiles of the formations. With simple cameras, stay within about nine feet of your subject. There are no special tours for photographers, as at Carlsbad Caverns, and no tripods are permitted underground. There are many photo subjects on the surface area of the national park, which covers 51,354 acres near Bowling Green, about one hundred miles from Louisville and the same distance from Nashville, Tennessee.

Picture-Taking Stops

You have a choice of several guided cave trips, for which a fee is charged, ranging from one and a half hours to all day. A good photographer's tour is the Echo River Trip, covering three miles in three hours. Your first picture should be of the group entering the natural opening, called the *Historic Entrance.*

Once within the *Rotunda,* a large chamber with forty-foot domed ceiling, you'll get good photos of leaching vats and wooden pipes used in saltpeter operations during the War of 1812. Long before then Indians penetrated the cave with reed torches to gather gypsum. The remains of one brave, believed to have been trapped more than two thousand years ago and now known as *Mummy John,* are displayed in a glass case; to avoid glare, take flash pictures at an angle to the glass.

The route leads down Broadway to the *Giant's Coffin,* an immense block weighing about two thousand tons. Nearby is the site of the world's first tubercular hospital, an ill-fated experiment of the 1840's, with remnants of two stone buildings still standing. In the lower area of unusual pits and domes, the trip visits the Bottomless Pit and Great Relief Hall, both too large to get a picture with one flash. However, gypsum flowers and formations are all over, some shaped like delicate petals and rosettes. Try to get a representative show of various forms of travertine: stalactites, stalagmites, columns, draperies, and flowstone.

At *Echo River,* 360 feet below the surface, the trip reaches the lowest depths of the cave open to visitors. Here you'll want to get a picture of the flat-bottom boat in which you cross the river, the largest underground stream in the cave. You may be able to get a picture of the famous blind fish. Then you go up past *Mammoth Dome,* the cave's highest known dome, returning to the Rotunda and the Historic Entrance.

On the all-day trip, you'll be able to see and photograph other impressive formations. *Frozen Niagara,* the most spectacular onyx formation, is too large to take in one picture, but you can get sections of fluted draperies and stalactites. A real treat is lunch at the *Snowball Room,* where the ceiling is adorned with gypsum snowballs. You may want to rest your camera firmly on a table and shoot a time exposure of a section of the room. The dining room has trash containers in which to dispose of used flashbulbs and empty film containers.

Above ground, in the scenic forested hills and valleys, a wide variety of wildflowers bloom in spring and summer, with swallowtail butterflies flitting among the butterflyweed. Whitetail deer, raccoon, woodchucks, and other animals make good subjects. In autumn the country is a blaze of color. You can see much of nature's best on the *Sunset Point Nature Trail,* which winds through the *Old Guides Cemetery* and along the river. "Miss Green River," a diesel-powered cruiser, makes several cruises daily, affording chances to spot deer, beaver, turkey, and a snake or two in their native habitat. The *evening campfire program* will fit well into your picture sequence and also provides a useful introduction to the park.

Nobody really knows how "mammoth" Mammoth Cave really is. It consists of many miles of charted passageways filled with spectacular formations, as well as uncounted miles that are still unexplored. Since its discovery in 1798, Mammoth Cave has been a favorite with tourists.

Mesa Verde National Park
Colorado 81330

High above the Four Corners, where Colorado, Utah, Arizona, and New Mexico meet, a vast, rocky tableland is honeycombed with deep canyons, where ancient Americans built apartment houses with balconies and terraces, great structures in the sheer rock encompassing entire villages. After thirteen hundred years, they wandered off to mingle with other tribes. But this national park memorializes their civilization and cultural achievements.

Mesa Verde represents a rendezvous of archaeology and nature, which the photographer can interpret through special attention to architecture. The dry climate and use of stone and adobe have combined to produce extremely well-preserved ruins. The four separate ages should be covered in pictures: the Basketmaker Period, when shallow caves furnished shelter; Modified Basketmaker Period, marked by development of the pithouse, a semisubterranean room with low wall and flat, mud-covered roof; Developmental Period, during which a rectangular structure with vertical side walls and true-course masonry emerged; and, finally, the Classic Pueblo Period, when nearly all house walls were double, and the great architectural monuments were constructed in the most spectacular locations on the cliff ledges and in the caves.

The cliff dwellings are best photographed from canyon-rim overlooks in the afternoon, for most caves face west-southwest. Large mesa-top ruins are good at any time of day. A telephoto lens will help in shooting distant dwellings, and a wide-angle lens when you are within the rooms. Mesa Verde covers 52,074 acres in the southwestern tip of Colorado, ten miles east of Cortez and thirty-eight miles west of Durango.

Picture-Taking Stops

When you enter the park, a twenty-mile drive leads to the main attractions. From the entrance you should shoot the towering escarpment of Point Lookout. Then take advantage of the overlooks along the way in order to depict the countryside the early dwellers knew. If you stay at the Morfield Canyon campground, five miles from the park entrance, you'll have plenty of chance to pick your locations and times of day. *Mancos* and *Montezuma Valley Overlooks* provide outstanding vistas of valley and mountains. *Park Point Fire Lookout,* the highest elevation in the park (8,572 feet), faces the vast horizons of Arizona, Utah, New Mexico, and Colorado. The mighty landmark of the desert, *Shiprock,* on the Navajo Indian Reservation, rises fourteen hundred feet. It makes a great vista at sunset, shimmering in the alpenglow.

The *Park Museum* makes an interesting stop for several reasons. It is in typical Southwest pueblo style. It was built as a gift from John D. Rockefeller, Jr., following his visit here in 1924. It contains a series of dioramas, accompanied by baskets, feather cloaks, jewels, and mummies found during excavations, which make clear the successive cultures of the cliff dwellers. Here you learn that the irreplaceable cliff dwellings are visited only when rangers are on duty; the mesa-top ruins may be visited unaccompanied.

During the summer, visitors can take a self-guided tour of the *Spruce Tree House,* the best-preserved large cliff dwelling in the park. Photograph it first from a distance on the canyon rim, showing the huge natural cave of weathered sandstone, before moving close up. The *Cliff Palace,* Mesa Verde's largest village, can be shown in stark beauty with shadows filling the crevices in the vaulted cave roof around the houses that rise four stories in some sections.

Guided trips are conducted to the impregnable *Balcony House* in Soda Canyon. You can take pictures of members of your party climbing ladders, walking along a narrow ledge, then crawling through the Needle's Eye, a small opening. At Balcony House an adobe-paved court spreads beneath a vaulted roof. On three sides stand beautifully built two-story houses, while along the fourth is the sheer cliff.

Two self-guiding loops on Ruins Road Drive provide views of many cliff dwellings with roofs still intact after a thousand years. One of the most striking, *Square Tower House,* rises to a height of four stories, built against the near-perpendicular wall of Navajo Canyon. *Sun Temple* is another highlight to be photographed from different angles; this great ceremonial structure of the late Classic Period, built in a D-shape, stands unroofed and unfinished, representing the mysterious end of the Mesa Verde civilization.

Mesa Verde is a rocky tableland where an ancient American civilization built its homes among the cliffs of sheer rock. Because the dwellings were built of stone and situated in such a dry climate, they are very well preserved. This park provides an adventure in archaeology and American history.

Mount McKinley National Park
P.O. Box 9
McKinley Park, Alaska 99755

The highest mountain on the North American continent, towering 20,320 feet above sea level, is the focal point of the northernmost—and second largest—national park, which lies only two hundred and fifty miles below the Arctic Circle. The park is preeminent also as a wildlife sanctuary and in this respect ranks with the world-famous preserves of South Africa. Two species of mammals are unique in the National Park System—Dall sheep and barren-ground caribou—but one finds them in company with a host of others, large and small, from snowshoe hare and hoary marmot to wolf, grizzly bear, and moose.

One of the nation's foremost wildlife photographers, Charles J. Ott, lives and works year-round in Mount McKinley National Park. If you study his classic pictures, of lynx, in particular, you can understand that the key to his approach is respect for his subject—he never disturbs an animal in its habitat, but exercises patience to show it in its true form.

Patience is a must in McKinley. During June and July up to twenty-one hours of daylight provide plenty of time for photography, but days are often cloudy, and perhaps half the time the mountain will be obscured. But you can use the weather to advantage. Cloudy days can be excellent for wildflower photography, so when McKinley and distant scenics are out of the question, turn your eyes downward to four hundred species of wildflowers. June and July are best, but wildflower displays range from the last snows of spring to first snows of winter. In late August, hill and tundra blaze with brilliant crimson, yellow, and gold. Forests of white spruce and cottonwood cling to semifrozen soil. Fireweed, aster, and larkspur huddle in bright patches.

Picture-Taking Stops

A single road extends ninety miles from its connection with the Denali Highway to the old mining settlement of Kantishna. Along the way are convenient turnoffs for wildlife-watching and picture-taking, with plenty of chances for hikes on gravel bars and dry ridges.

The park terrain rises from about fourteen hundred feet to the summit of Mount McKinley. Near the gateway to the park, in the McKinley Park Hotel area, walk the *Horseshoe Lake Trail.* Fine views of the spruce-lined lake unfold at the overlook several hundred feet above. As you travel in the park, you'll become conscious of three life communities—the northern forest, tundra, and perennial snowfields—which you should try to interpret on film. In strips along the river bottoms the *northern forest,* or taiga, is composed largely of spruce, balsam poplar, and aspen, with black spruce in the muskeg, and many showy wildflowers, with wildlife including moose, lynx, and snowshoe hare. Watch for beavers during twilight hours; include shots of dams, a lodge, and tooth-marked aspen or willow.

At *milepost 9* you may get your first glimpse of the great mountain Denali, the climax of the Alaska Range, which extends six hundred miles across south-central Alaska in a vast band. It is part of the highest-elevation life community, unvegetated above five thousand feet, with *perennial snowfields* above eight thousand feet and great systems of glaciers on the south side, where precipitation is greatest. Spruces at the roadside make a fine frame for pictures. Many other places will offer views of the mountain, one of the finest being from Stony Hill overlook (milepost 61). Unobstructed panoramas of the mountain and adjacent ice-sheathed peaks will be continuously visible from Eielson Visitor Center (milepost 66) to Wonder Lake (milepost 86). At least once during your visit, plan to photograph the alpenglow at sunset and again at sunrise a few hours later.

Teklanika River (milepost 27) typifies glacial streams, flowing over wide gravel bars. The willow thickets around Hogan Creek-Sanctuary-Teklanika are good places to photograph moose. In August bulls are most photogenic, with their full antler spread. In the *Sable Pass area* (mileposts 37-42) photographers and hikers are prohibited from leaving the road, in order to protect both themselves and the wildlife. But this offers an excellent opportunity to photograph grizzly bears with telephoto lens (the only safe way). The *tundra life community* ranges in elevation from three thousand to five thousand feet, with vegetation composed largely of sedges, mosses, and lichens; abundant members of the heath family, such as blueberries, Labrador tea, and low-bush cranberry, make good photographic subjects. Distinctive animals are associated with the tundra. As you drive in the *Toklat River country* and past the Muldrow Glacier, large herds of caribou often can be seen, particularly in June and early July, when they are in migration. Only a few can be seen along the road during the peak of summer, but they again appear in late August; at this period they are most photogenic, with full-grown antlers and light cape of the bulls most pronounced. Scan the hillsides north of the road with binoculars for a band of Dall sheep, white-cloaked lords of the high country; a photo of these animals will be a prize.

From *Eielson Visitor Center,* you can shoot Muldrow Glacier and the towering twin peaks. If you drive slowly and keep a sharp eye, you may be rewarded with a chance to see and photograph a wolf or wolverine, exceptional animals of the wild, both shy creatures and far from numerous. You may spot a porcupine climbing to the top of a willow to feed on young shoots. Foxes become fairly tame in the park and frequently are seen hunting parka squirrels along the roadsides at dusk. Don't overlook the birds, which range up to the powerful golden eagle, one of nature's most splendid creatures. The willow ptarmigan, which typifies the North country, can usually be seen prospecting along the road. June is the best month for birds; populations are large, and many of the 132 recorded species are in breeding plumage.

Near the northern boundary of the park, *Wonder Lake* makes a fitting climax for your visit. Magnificent pictures can be made here, with the mountain reflection in the lake. One of Alaska's top photographers, Ginny Hill Wood, is especially noted for her Wonder Lake shots. She is co-owner of Camp Denali, a wilderness camp just outside the boundary, which features wildlife-photography sessions.

Mount Rainier National Park
Longmire, Washington 98397

The towering volcanic cone, gleaming with glacial ice, rises 14,410 feet high, as a monumental natural landmark of the Pacific Northwest and as the core of a vibrant life community. The Wonderland Trail, which completely encircles the mountain for ninety miles, undoubtedly is one of the most fascinating single trails in the entire National Park System. The full trip takes about ten days, yet one can spend as little as half a day doing a portion of it—or even thirty minutes on one of the self-guiding nature trails.

Photographic opportunities are limitless, though you must expect misty days and learn to make the most of them. The features you interpret should cover: *grand views of the mountain,* soaring above its base more than any other in the forty-eight lower states; *views of the glaciers,* with some portions readily accessible and others testing the hardiest climber; *superlative forest scenes* in the moisture-rich valleys; *wildflowers,* extending through several life zones from snowbanks to the deep woods; *lakes, streams, and waterfalls; wild animals* in their native habitat, including beaver, coyote, hoary marmots in rock-slide dwellings, and mountain goats above timberline; and the *human visitor,* conquering a summit, hiking a trail, fishing a wilderness stream, or fixing a campfire.

Mount Rainier, like almost any national park, is worth sampling and photographing in fall, winter, and spring as well as summer. At no time from early spring to early autumn can you fail to find a flower display somewhere in the park. Indian-summer weather sometimes continues well into October, when the season is enlivened by the bright red of mountain-ash berries, the brilliant reds of vine maples, and other colors.

Your choice of film may be dictated by weather. Come prepared with high-speed film for dark days, since the concession store carries only popular types. Before you arrive you may want to get some picture ideas by reviewing some of the books on the region with illustrations by Bob and Ira Spring, master outdoor photographers of the Pacific Northwest, such as "100 Hikes in Western Washington," by Louise B. Marshall; "Trips and Trails," by E. M. Sterling; and "High Worlds of the Mountain Climber," by the Spring brothers themselves. If you would like to get aerial photographs, scenic flights are available from Ashford, outside the park, and the pilot is obliging about placing photographers in position for good pictures.

Picture-Taking Stops

Many visitors arrive through the southwest gateway, the Nisqually Entrance. About one mile inside the boundary, a forest of Douglas fir, western hemlock, western red cedar, and Sitka spruce typifies the monarchs of the Northwest, some of which live five hundred years or longer, towering taller than fifteen-story buildings. Swordfern, ladyfern, bracken, and deerfern form part of the forest floor and can be pictured as dwarf forests. About two hundred species of fungi in the forest have colorful fruiting bodies in the fall.

Shoot such subjects and flowers *in place*, as part of their natural community. If they are in shadow, you can often light them by using mirrors or foil to reflect the sunlight or take advantage of diffused light on overcast days.

Instead of taking the main road, you can turn north and make a photographic expedition along the forested *West Side Road*, which is open in summer only. It affords a good chance to see wildlife and to get outstanding pictures many visitors miss. *Gobblers Knob Trail* makes a fine hike past Lake George to the lookout, with superior views of the mountain and surrounding terrain. Many views of Rainier will require wide-angle lens to capture the scope of the scene. The road extends thirteen miles from its beginning to *Klapatche Point*, another good vantage point for photographing the mountain panorama. Several trails lead from the road up to Wonderland Trail. One follows the South Puyallup River up to *Emerald Ridge*, within range of the leading edge of Tahoma Glacier. This is good country to observe and photograph the finest mountaineers of the park—the handsomely adapted mountain goats.

The main road from the Nisqually Entrance leads up the Nisqually Valley to park headquarters at Longmire. The trail to *Eagle Peak*, at elevation 5,955 feet, though rather steep, is rewarded with magnificent photo possibilities, not only of Mount Rainier but also of Mount St. Helens, Mount Adams, and occasionally Mount Hood to the south. Beyond the Cougar Rock campground, the Van Trump Park Trail leads to *Comet Falls*, one of the highest and most beautiful in the park.

The Paradise Visitor Center is the gateway to many activities, including guided walks during the summer and snowshoeing, skiing, and sledding during the winter. One of the best photo trips is on the *Nisqually Glacier Vista Trail*, which begins in a wildflower meadow, then climbs upward to a viewpoint above the ice of Nisqually, one of the largest, longest, and most active glaciers. Note that off-trail travel, especially on glaciers, is hazardous and requires technical training and proper equipment. Concession-guided trips of 2 1/2 miles are conducted every day during the summer to the *Paradise Glacier Ice Caves*, vast tubes beneath the glacier, where the daylight is refracted as a deep blue. This is the only trail in the park which takes the average hiker (not specifically dressed for travel on glaciers) right to a glacier, where he may even get out on the ice in safety. The guide service conducts a varied program for novices and trained climbers. Spectacular pictures are possible on the one-day trip, and far more so in the five-day school which culminates in a climb over ice and rock to the summit of Mount Rainier.

For those continuing east by car from Paradise, the Stevens Canyon Road passes beautiful Reflection and Louise lakes, with vistas of the rugged Tatoosh Range and Mount Adams. The hike to *Pinnacle Peak* is rewarded with flower displays and a classic portrait of Mount Rainier above the forests. An even shorter trail leads up to *Bench Lake* and *Snow Lake*, two lovely spots at the foot of Unicorn Peak.

On the east side of the park, the Ohanapecosh Visitor Center is the gateway to splendid forest and water scenery. The *Silver Falls Trail* loops through a Douglas-fir and hemlock forest along the Ohanapecosh River to Silver Falls, one of the park's loveliest cascades. This is good elk country, especially in autumn. Upriver, near the Stevens Canyon Entrance, the *Grove of the Patriarchs* self-guiding trail leads through a grove of some of the largest and oldest living trees in the Pacific Northwest. Photograph the trailside markers as titles for your picture sequence.

Driving north along the east side of the park, the three-mile side trip from Cayuse Pass to Tipsoo Lake and Chinook Pass is well worth the effort. Tipsoo is ringed with Cascadian flowers during the brief "springtime," which make a lovely foreground for Rainier. Short trails lead to scenic spots and viewpoints.

The *Mather Memorial Highway*, named for the first director of the National Park Service, continues north, a boulevard lined by forest giants in the White River Valley. Following the river on the road to the Sunrise area, you'll get a whole new perspective. Look for the outcroppings of andesite columns that once flowed from Rainier volcano; they make interesting patterns on film. *Sunrise Point* opens sweeping roadside views. From Sunrise, the highest point reached by car in the park (elevation 6,400 feet), many nature trails and short hikes lead to dramatic scenic locations. The *Emmons Glacier Vista* embraces a wide sweep from the mountain summit down through the ice fields of the largest glacier in the park to the reaches of the White River. *Sourdough Mountain Trail* offers a continuing flower show from late June through September. *Huckleberry Creek Trail* up to Forest Lake follows a clear-water stream through log jams and over rocks, with good views of the mountain. You can also take off from here for an overnight hike on the Wonderland Trail, heading up Berkeley Park and past Skyscraper Mountain for pictures of Winthrop Glacier and Mystic Lake; then you can continue past Carbon Glacier, one of the principal active glaciers of Mount Rainier, noted for the

Willis Wall, and head down to Ipsut Creek campground, where you can have friends pick you up via the Carbon River Entrance.

The Carbon River country, still relatively unspoiled, is marked by virgin forests, in which you can photograph decaying fallen giants serving as nurse-logs for young trees, part of the patient continuation of life forms. If you drive up the Mowich Lake Road, you can hike past *Eunice Lake*, which reflects the spectacular western slope of Mount Rainier in its waters, to *Tolmie Peak Lookout*, noted for its sweeping panoramic views. A longer trail leads to *Spray Park*, where snowfields are likely to be found even in late summer, and Spray Falls. The open alpine meadows, vast flower fields, and superb views both challenge and inspire the photographer to capture the wilderness freedom of Mount Rainier.

Mount Rainier's towering volcanic cone, gleaming with glacial ice, is a magnificent natural landmark of the Pacific Northwest. You can explore and camp along the ninety-miles of fascinating Wonderland Trails, which completely encircle the mountain.

North Cascades National Park
Sedro Woolley, Washington 98284

Deep, rugged precipices rise sharply above the dense rain forests. A concentration of more than one hundred and fifty glaciers feeds innumerable creeks, waterfalls, mountain lakes, and free-flowing rivers. The mountain slopes are clothed with wild gardens. These are some of the qualities of the "Wilderness Alps of America," which became a national park in 1968.

Much of the North Cascades is still pristine, barely scarred, and little known outside the state of Washington, but the mountains rank easily among the prime scenic areas of the country. Portions already are accessible, since the Cascades formerly were administered by the U.S. Forest Service, especially for wilderness fishing, hunting, and trail travel. Two portions, Ross Lake National Recreation Area and Lake Chelan National Recreation Area, will still be open to hunting, but the entire 670,000-acre complex is open to hunting-with-camera. Weather will be a major challenge, so prepare to work with elements of mist and moisture.

Picture-Taking Stops

In general, low-elevation areas are densely timbered, good for shooting pictures of ruffed grouse, deer, forests, and tumbling streams. But it's often difficult to see high peaks from the road because of the prominent front ridge, and you can expect to hike or ride the trails for a vantage point facing some of the spectacular scenery.

As an introduction to the north unit of the park, you can drive to *Ross Lake* and take a boat trip toward the Canadian border. You'll get interesting patterns of snowy peaks reflected in the water while passing the inlets of clear streams like Little Beaver Creek. On the west rise the peaks of the mighty Pickett Range, the heart of the wilderness in this part of the park. Farther north you'll get shots of Little Jackass Mountain and the Canadian peaks beyond the head of the lake.

The Skagit River empties from Ross Lake into *Diablo Lake*, where the boat cruise offers access into the heart of the North Cascades. Then you can go on foot from Colonial Creek campground to a variety of areas. A short hike leads to *Sourdough Mountain*, looking up at towering peaks and glaciers in motion. Contrary to popular belief, most of this country can be hiked, but the rugged ridges that cut up the country are not to be tried except by those with a rock-climbing background. North from here, you can go up Big Beaver Creek to *Whatcom Pass* and the high lakes—this trip does not require rock-climbing experience. Neither does the shorter hike to *Ruby Mountain*.

Diablo Lake lies between the north and south units of the new park. An impressive trip to the south—not strenuous, but two to three days for most walkers—leads up *Thunder Creek*, over *Park Creek Pass*, and down to Lake Chelan. This trip passes close to spectacular glaciers and the lofty, beautifully proportioned peaks of the Eldorado wilderness—such as Eldorado, Forbidden, Buckner, and Goode. You should be able to photograph mountain goats on the rocky crags; Washington's goat population is exceeded only by those in Montana and Alaska.

An alternative to the above route is to drive from the west to Marblemount on the Skagit River, then twenty-two miles along the Cascade River, stopping two miles short of *Cascade Pass* in the scenic climax of the range. The short hike to the pass takes one through an alpine world of flower meadows, sheer cliffs, a chain of magnificently glaciered peaks, and the headwaters of two wild rivers flowing east and west. Cascade Pass is one of the most popular areas; the trail down to Lake Chelan may have up to one hundred people at a time on the weekend.

Another access to the south unit is from Chelan by boat or float plane. You can create a picture story from the time you board the passenger ferry and ride up the fifty-five-mile-long lake. The strange canyon of Lake Chelan, with a total of nine thousand feet from mountain summit to lake bottom, is one of the deepest in the world. The head of Lake Chelan at *Stehekin* is the gateway to many trips into the park wilderness.

The cliff dwellings of Mesa Verde provide a lesson in Indian history. You'll get a lot of exercise climbing around the Cliff Palace shown here. For the brightest color, photograph the cliff dwellings when they're illuminated by the afternoon sun. In the morning and on overcast days, the dwellings take on a softer, "quiet" look.

MOUNT McKINLEY

The low angle of the sun creates warm highlights on the snowy peaks of Mount McKinley, while the dark foreground and clouds add a quiet mood to the scene. Lighting is constantly changing as the sun moves across the sky. You can create an interesting picture series by photographing the same subject at different times of day.

Part of the Alaskan Range towers in the background, and the figures at the lower left balance the composition and provide a contrast to the massive mountain. Wherever you go, be sure to snap plenty of pictures to share your trip with the folks at home.

The sun seems to dance on the surface of Wonder Lake at the foot of Mount McKinley. You may need a lot of patience to photograph this view because oftentimes the fog doesn't lift off the mountain until late in the day.

MOUNT RAINIER

The hills in Mt. Rainier Park are dotted with pine and dressed in winter white. The graceful curving shoreline of the lake gently directs the viewer's attention toward the center of the scene. You can photograph many scenes such as this from your car!

Pictures of wildlife add variety to your travel photographs. For the most interesting pictures, move as close as you can to your main subject, or use a telephoto lens, and try to fill your picture area with the subject. This close-up is more dramatic than a picture taken from a distance and showing the whole deer.

The Visitor's Center in Olympic National Park provides many scenic views of Lake Crescent and Pyramid Mountain. Here the photographer carefully selected his viewpoint to capture the lake framed by the center's rustic porch.

Light and shadows play over bands of sandstone, shale, and clay in a variety of hues. This park ranges from towering mesas to flat expanses of desert. Before taking a picture, make sure the camera strap is not over the lens and check to see that your fingers are not covering the exposure meter of an automatic camera.

As Travertine Creek winds its way through Platt National Park it creates many a pastoral scene such as this. Show imagination in your vacation picture-taking by photographing interesting or colorful reflections in peaceful streams and lakes.

For a simple, uncluttered background in your pictures, use a low viewpoint and photograph your subjects against the sky. This oddly shaped tree is part of a forest which burned in 1900. The winds in this area are so strong that branches grow only on one side of the tree.

Looking across the placid waters of Bear Lake, you can see Long's Peak, in the far background, and the Keyboard to the Winds. A bright sweater or jacket should be a standard part of any photo enthusiast's traveling gear. You'll never be sorry you have one along to add color to any scene.

You can see Long's Peak from Moriane Park Campground. Take pictures of the places where you stay to add a "we were there" feeling to your picture story.

You'll enjoy your close-up pictures of beautiful wild flowers, such as this columbine. You can get inexpensive close-up lenses for any camera.

The rangers say that there's enough wood in the General Sherman Tree to make a box large enough to hold the "Queen Elizabeth," and there probably would be enough wood left over to make a lid! When you photograph large subjects, such as the General Sherman Tree, include a person in the picture for size comparison.

In many national parks, the rangers hold regularly scheduled tours for visitors. During these tours, the rangers will point out unusual natural sights that the untrained eye might miss. There is usually time for picture-taking on these tours. Be sure to take your camera and extra film.

To give the folks back home a glimpse of the beauty which abounds in our national parks, take some close-up pictures of the many interesting leaves and wild flowers you'll see. For this picture, the photographer selected a low viewpoint so the sun shining through the leaves shows off their translucent beauty, then he moved in for a close-up view to get the maximum amount of detail.

VIRGIN ISLANDS

Here is a tropical paradise with clear aquamarine bays, wide white sandy beaches, and lush rolling hills. You'll see many breathtaking scenes to photograph. For the best quality in your pictures, keep your film and camera out of hot places such as automobile glove compartments, and have the film processed as soon as possible.

YELLOWSTONE

Top left. The animals in the parks are fascinating picture subjects. This bull moose was so busy feeding on plants in the Yellowstone River that he didn't notice he was being photographed.

Center. Colorful lichen grows profusely in Yellowstone. Close-up pictures record the detail and color of the lichen, one of the smallest forms of plant life.

Lower left. Keep your camera handy so you won't miss the unexpected subjects like this beaver feeding on a water lily. Move quietly; don't frighten him away.

Right. Tower Falls thunders 132 feet down into the canyon. In summer, photograph the falls at midday when the sun is high overhead illuminating the falls.

A foreground of pines makes a natural frame which gives this picture a feeling of depth. You can photograph this view of Vernal Falls, at the lower left, and Nevada Falls, at the upper right, from Washburn Point.

Whether you take this picture at high noon or in the evening, when the sun is sinking behind the mountains, you're sure to get a striking photograph of the famous Jeffrey Pine on top of Sentinel Dome. This is one of most photographed trees in the world!

A fire in the center of the tree created an unusual shape out of this giant which is known as the Clothespin Tree. You can emphasize the split in the tree in your pictures by shooting from a low angle and aiming straight up the tree trunk.

Top. In the narrow, curving gorge of Zion Canyon, nature has carved and painted sandstone and shale cliffs and temples. Include people in your pictures to show the scale of these huge cliffs.

Lower left. Information signs are a common sight in the parks. These signs make excellent titles for your travel pictures. The signs also provide historical and geographical information for future reference.

Lower right. Move in close —ouch! Well, not *that* close, but near enough to get a picture which shows in sharp detail the spines on this cactus—or the petals of the flowers you'll want to photograph in the park.

Olympic National Park
Port Angeles, Washington 98362

This national park in the upper corner of Washington State embraces the finest remaining wilderness rain forest of a type that once paralleled the Pacific from California to Alaska. The lush virgin woodlands in the western valleys are links of the interacting chain of life zones extending from the glacial ice and saw-toothed peaks of the Olympic Mountains down through slopes covered with flowering meadows to a fifty-mile primitive coastline, where swift-flowing streams rejoin the sea.

But the area first came into prominence because of its wildlife, notably the Olympic, or Roosevelt, elk. The largest remaining herd of this species lives in the park, together with the Olympic marmot and certain other small animal forms found only in these mountain fastnesses.

The park covers 896,599 acres on the Olympic Peninsula. The west side is wet—more rain falls on the lower slopes than in any other part of the contiguous United States—and photographers must adjust to it, both in clothing and exposure.

Picture-Taking Stops

The most accessible portions of the park lie along the north side. Starting from the Pioneer Memorial Museum at Port Angeles, the scenic Heart o' the Hills Road leads eighteen miles from sea level to almost a mile high. At Lookout Rock, about halfway up, you can photograph the panorama of Juan de Fuca Strait, extending north to Canada. *Hurricane Ridge* offers an infinite variety of views of high, glacial-carved peaks, including Mount Olympus, on which seven glaciers are born, their ice extending for thirty miles or more. The mountain meadows along the ridge are carpeted with flowers from late June, when the first lilies rise through retreating snow, until October, when crimson and gold signal the autumn season. The honey-brown Olympic marmots are common. Hikers taking the trail to nearby *Mount Angeles* should be able to get pictures of mountain goats and black-tailed deer. A scenic road, fittingly called the Alpine Drive, leads to Obstruction Point, with the best view of Olympus available by road. This is the start of many hiking trails, including the popular route to *Deer Park*, with coastal vistas to the north and mountain views to the south.

Lake Crescent, one of the most beautiful lakes in the park, also lies on the north side and is easily reached by car. Throughout the year the deep blue lake wears many moods, from the mistlike freshness of a bright spring day to the troubled waters of a driving winter storm. The beauty of Marymere Falls can be enjoyed after a short walk from Storm King Visitor Center. In late spring you may get pictures of wild mallard ducks from U.S. 101, which follows the south shore. At the western end of the lake, a road leaves U.S. 101 and penetrates a beautiful forest to Sol Duc Hot Springs. This is the start of the trail up to the snow-covered cirque of *Seven Lakes Basin* and the *High Divide*, with a chance to photograph Mount Olympus at closer range.

In the Pacific Coast area of the park, forest-fringed beaches and wave-lashed islands are the setting of LaPush, a fishing village where Quileute Indians can still be seen setting fish nets from old dugout canoes. Just to the north, at *Rialto Beach,* the photographer can walk along pebbly, gray beaches and record the pounding surf meeting the land. Great piles of drift logs line the high-water mark. Farther south, off U.S. 101, *Ruby Beach* in the Hoh Indian Reservation has many islets, or seastacks, and sea arches to delight the eye. At *Kalaloch,* the road hugs the cliff and offers glimpses of ocean through the trees. Short trails lead to the beach, a rendezvous of life between the tides, with colorful sea urchins and anemones thriving where the shore is rocky and protected from strong waves. Along these beaches you can see many types of wildlife, from these tidepool creatures to beach-walking bears, migrating whales, frolicking seals, and a great host of birds.

The finest temperate-climate rain forests in the world are located in the Quinault, Queets, and Hoh valleys. Most moisture falls from late autumn to early spring; summer is comparatively dry, with many clear, sunny days. The large forest trees, reaching as high as two hundred feet, attract most attention, but the ground cover of flowering plants, mosses, and ferns offers a fragile beauty to the camera. The bigleaf maple is prime habitat for luxurious drooping growths of airplants such as club moss and licorice fern, which have a translucent appearance in the sunlight. Hoh Valley is the most accessible of the rain forests, with two self-guiding nature trails looping from the Visitor Center. Here one can follow the story of a fallen forest giant through a series of plant successions, once again leading to a towering, moss-covered Sitka spruce or Douglas fir.

The photographer should also sample the rugged eastern side of the park. For instance, the road to *Dosewallips,* off U.S. 101 south of Quilcene, opens vistas deep into the ridges and valleys of the high Olympics. You can follow trails past Dose Cascades to alpine *Lake Constance,* rimmed by mountain peaks.

From the glacial ice and sawtoothed peaks of the Olympic Mountains, through the flowering meadows, down to the fifty-mile coastline, Olympic National Park is a spectacular wilderness which supports the largest remaining herd of Olympic elk.

Petrified Forest National Park
Holbrook, Arizona 86025

Northern Arizona looked much different one hundred and sixty million years ago. In place of the weirdly eroded and arid badlands of today, the area then was a swampy lowland, where shifting streams spread across vast flood plains. Clusters of pine-like trees were swept up by flood, then buried under sand and mud. Ground water picked up silica and other minerals in the deposits and infused them into the wood cells, turning them, over a course of centuries, into the world's biggest, brightest collections of petrified wood.

Preserving a bridge to the past, shattered stone trees glow with rainbow colors. Thousands of great logs lie scattered about; here and there the ground is strewn with slabs and chips, still true to the details of the original wood. In the heart of the stark Painted Desert, this national park preserves 94,189 acres from souvenir hunters and commercial collectors so that future generations may continue to enjoy these treasures of nature. It is one of the favorite objectives of nature photographers in the Southwest. In May and June, wildflowers are in bloom, including mariposa, paintbrush, prickly pear, and globemallow, adding the desert's living touch to the forest of fallen stone.

Picture-Taking Stops

The special features of the park are linked by paved roads. As you travel through, remember that federal law prohibits removal of any petrified wood, no matter how small. Trash containers for film boxes and wrappers are available along the way.

Entering at the north, a loop from the Visitor Center faces the amazing plateaus, buttes, and low mesas of the *Painted Desert*. Several viewpoints afford vantages for spectacular scenery, including Pilot Rock, the highest point in the park. Colors ranging from gaudy red to soft blue are most vivid after a rain. Early or late in the day are the best times for pictures, because shadows provide contrast, and the warmer light intensifies the red colors of the soil. If you are conditioned to the desert, you may want to hike to the roadless section called Black Forest, a concentration of dark petrified wood—be sure to check with a ranger first.

South on the park road, the *Puerco Indian Ruin* consists of remains of walls at the site of an Indian settlement occupied six centuries ago. These early desert dwellers recorded their presence with hundreds of primitive symbols in *Newspaper Rock*, a huge sandstone block. When you photograph this link with the past, include a member of your party examining the petroglyphs to indicate the size of the rock.

At *Blue Mesa*, colorful banded buttes, mesas, and cones clearly reveal the ancient layers of marsh. Erosion nibbling at the soft earth has left some petrified logs stranded in unusual postures on slender pedestals. Other outstanding features are found at the *Tepees, Agate Bridge, Jasper Forest, Crystal Forest,* and *Flattops.*

Rainbow Forest, an extensive area near the south entrance, is a major point of interest. Many trunks exceed one hundred feet in length, while the Old Faithful Log, a sprawling monster near the museum, has the largest base diameter of any tree readily seen. The Long Logs self-guiding trail shows excellent examples of fossil wood in the remains of an ancient logjam. A partially restored pueblo, the Agate House, built centuries ago of petrified wood chunks, overlooks the Rainbow Forest at the end of a foot trail. Polished-wood sections exhibited at the museum show to best advantage the varied color pattern. The Rainbow Forest Visitor Center Museum contains displays explaining the riddles of the "stone trees."

In the Petrified Forest, thousands of great stone trees flowing with a rainbow of colors comprise the world's biggest and brightest collection of petrified wood. In May and June, when the wild flowers are in bloom, nature adds a living touch to the forest of fallen stone.

Platt National Park

P.O. Box 201
Sulphur, Oklahoma 73086

The smallest national park covers 912 acres, an oasis in the prairies, with interesting biological, geological, and historical features. The rolling hills and valleys offer examples of two distinct plant associations. The valleys, lower slopes, and some hills are wooded with an eastern hardwood forest. But many upper slopes and hilltops are examples of the prairies more typical of the West.

Picture-Taking Stops

You can start at the Visitor Center and then head for *Bromide Hill* by road or trail. The hill offers a vantage point for overall views of both prairie and forest, with the Arbuckle Mountains along the horizon to the southwest. Every morning during summer a naturalist leads a nature walk from the museum to the summit. This outing offers many interesting picture possibilities. You can include other members of your party in your pictures. Because of the proximity of the city of Sulphur, most views from the hilltop are likely to include urban or farming areas. If you want to include only natural scenery in your pictures, choose your viewpoint carefully.

Antelope Springs, a large freshwater spring, flows in the east end of the park, a quiet reminder of the days when antelope herds came down from the prairie for water. Together with Buffalo Springs it forms the source of *Travertine Creek,* a pleasant tree-shaded stream with attractive small pools and waterfalls. Scenes of sunlight streaming through the overhanging trees offer interesting potential for pictures; colors are especially brilliant in autumn, with an inter-mingling of the red and scarlet of oaks with the gold and yellow of cottonwoods.

Throughout the park, from early spring to late fall, there are many opportunities for close-ups of individual flowers, moss-covered travertine rocks—a type of porous, spongy limestone—and, occasionally, small animals such as the raccoon, opossum, bobcat, armadillo, squirrel, and sleek gray fox. A series of such pictures could result in a fine portrayal of the varying environments here.

The eight-mile *Perimeter Drive* gives different scenic views of the park features. When you return to the museum you may want to ask someone to take a picture of you at *Bromide Pavilion,* where waters of the mineral springs are dispensed.

Redwood National Park
Crescent City, California 95531

The earth's tallest known living trees are now preserved in this national park established by Congress in 1968, culminating a ninety-year-long crusade to achieve federal status for the majestic *Sequoia sempervirens.* The 58,000-acre park embraces a forty-five-mile-long stretch of forest and unspoiled beach in the extreme northwest corner of California. Of these lands, 38,000 acres have been publicly held for up to forty years in three California state parks, which are scheduled to become part of the new national park. These offer miles of trails under towering giants.

The great coastal redwoods are found only in this region, where moisture approaches the proportions of a rain forest. The coastal redwood resembles its cousin, the giant sequoia, or *Sequoia gigantea,* which grows in the Sierra Nevadas, but differs from it in key respects. The coastal redwood is taller, with slender trunk, while the giant sequoia has an immense trunk and very slight taper. As you travel the national parks, photographing big trees in this area and in Yosemite and Sequoia-Kings Canyon, try to capture other differences in the barks, leaves, limbs, and cones.

Picture-Taking Stops

The southern boundary of the park lies near Orick, a small town close to the Pacific Ocean and three hundred and thirty miles north of San Francisco. Six miles north of town, *Prairie Creek State Park* (which is being incorporated into the national park) presents a superb botanical garden, combining great coastal redwoods, Douglas fir, western hemlock, and Sitka spruce, knitted together with broad-leafed trees and many flowering plants. The redwood forest should be viewed as a plant community, including fern, trillium, and small herbs that lend a magic quality to the total system. Along *Fern Canyon* on the Irvine Trail you'll be able to photograph the beautiful and varied banks of fern.

In a meadow and open woods a herd of two hundred Roosevelt elk roam free and unfenced. They make splendid picture subjects, but avoid getting too close—for your own good. The park ranges in elevation from fifteen hundred feet to sea level. The western slopes drop off abruptly at the *Gold Bluffs,* fronting the Pacific. Here you can get unusual pictures of sand flecked with gold, rugged promontories, and huge waves breaking on the rocks.

Southeast of the state park, on Redwood Creek, the *Emerald Mile* contains a concentration of the world's tallest trees, one giant reaching 367.4 feet. This stand is located on private land to be included in the national park, along with the heavily wooded watershed of Lost Man Creek. For the past two years the lumber company owning the tract has encouraged tours through the area, known as Tall Trees Grove.

Driving north on U.S. 101, the Redwood Highway passes through many miles of redwoods. In taking pictures of the big trees along the way, get the sun behind you and include a car coming or going to illustrate relative size, preferably a red car (or some other bright color) for contrast.

Six miles north of the town of Klamath, the road enters *Del Norte Coast Redwoods State Park*. Trails lead through four outstanding groves, with many trees growing to the edge of the seven-mile-long rocky ocean shore. May and June are choice months for picture-taking, with huge banks of blooming rhododendron and azalea enlivening the woods.

The park has its northern boundary on the beautiful Smith River. You can get excellent scenic views at the confluence of the Smith and Mill creeks, both fast, white-water streams with many deep pools. In late afternoon you might see river otters at work and play. In the fall, fishermen try their luck for steelhead and salmon, running up to thirty pounds, adding another dimension to pictures. Along Mill Creek, in *Jedediah Smith State Park,* some of the finest redwoods are found. Because of its location at the eastern edge of the coast redwood belt, this park contains an interesting combination of coastal and inland trees, including ponderosa pines, with a lush underbrush of rhododendron, azalea, fern, oxalis, salal, and huckleberry. The *Stout Memorial Grove* contains the largest trees in the park, including the 340-foot Stout Tree, a giant among giants. The loop on Old Stagecoach Road, wide enough for one car, will afford many opportunities for pictures in a misty setting.

Rocky Mountain National Park
Estes Park, Colorado 80517

Perpetual snows cloak the highest summits and valley walls that rise over more than fourteen thousand feet, and small glaciers still exist at the heads of sheltered gorges. The sculptured ridges, needlelike crags, great cirques, and remote lakes are reminders of times past in the Colorado Rockies. The forests and wildflowers tell other stories—of struggle and adjustment to environments which differ with altitude and exposure.

People come from all corners of the world, and in all seasons, to view the spectacles of the park in the heart of the Front Range, the first wave of the Rockies to rise from the plains. Trail Ridge Road, which follows an ancient trail used by the Utes and Arapahoes, is one of America's best-known auto trips. It has few equals for sheer scenic beauty, easy access to the fantasies of timberline, interesting tundra, and variety of natural landscapes within a few miles. In addition, many hikes of varying lengths lead to scenic features on three hundred miles of trail.

The park covers 262,324 acres of varied high mountain country. A visit reminds one of the words written by Enos Mills, a prominent booster of the Rockies of half a century ago: "Within national parks is room—glorious room—room in which to find ourselves, in which to think and hope, to dream and plan, to rest and resolve."

Mornings are best for pictures, since most photogenic scenery faces the east, and afternoons may be cloudy. Autumn is a period of clear days, when aspens glitter golden on the slopes. Seasons are apt to be off-schedule in some years. Visitors coming to photograph spring wildflowers in April have been greeted by a snowstorm. Spring starts in May, and summer is over about mid-August, but the beautiful fall may extend to late October. Film, processing mailers, and other photographic supplies and equipment are available at Estes Park, Grand Lake, and other gateway communities.

Picture-Taking Stops

Approaching from Estes Park, the new *park headquarters* and Visitor Center should be your starting point. This beautiful low building of reddish-pink stone was designed by the Taliesen Group, associates of the late Frank Lloyd Wright. It makes a striking contrast with the strange "panorama" of signboards which confronts visitors outside the boundary. Chart your course here for your photo coverage of key features, which should include the following: lakes, streams, wildflowers, tundra, wildlife, and visitor activities.

One good photo route leads over the Bear Lake Road to Bear Lake, the only high lake in the park accessible by car. The *Moraine Park Visitor Center,* an early stop, is a choice place to see evidences of ancient glaciers, both on exhibit and from the observation porch; there are splendid views of Longs Peak, the highest mountain in the park. The road traverses glaciated meadows and moraines and will afford many chances to photograph Thatchtop Mountain and the stands of aspen on Bierstadt Ridge. At *Glacier Basin*

Campground you can photograph Otis Peak, Hallett's Peak, and the Tyndall Glacier, using pine trees in the foreground to frame your pictures.

Bear Lake, at the end of the road, nestles at the foot of high mountains, serving as a foreground for the view up Tyndall Gorge, with the sheer cliff of Hallett's Peak adding a dramatic background to this alpine scene. A half-mile foot trail encircles the lake, providing many opportunities for excellent scenic pictures. This is a self-guiding nature hike, with numbers along the trail that relate to a pamphlet available at the park. The pamphlet helps photographers identify what they photograph. From Bear Lake a hike of one mile leads to *Dream Lake,* near the foot of Hallett's Peak, with a matchless view up Tyndall Gorge. You can join the guided *Fern and Odessa Lakes* trip; it takes all day, but these two lakes are in one of the most beautiful canyons on the eastern side of the Continental Divide.

A second photo trip from park headquarters follows the one-way nine-mile-long old *Fall River Road,* narrow, winding, and completely safe if you stick to the fifteen-mile speed limit; it is intended for sightseeing and picture-taking at a leisurely pace. It joins the main road at Fall River Pass. At the start take long-range pictures of the Front Range. Use the parking overlooks to photograph Fall River and Horseshoe Park; an aspen grove will help to frame Mt. Ypsilon. Soon after starting up the Fall River Road, watch to your right for a large rounded pothole, probably drilled by stones in a whirlpool about the time of the last glacier. Park at the marked area for *Chasm Falls,* photographing the sign before following the short trail to the beautiful twenty-five-foot-high cascade. At its base, it too is slowly drilling a pothole, similar to the one you saw a few minutes ago.

Farther up the road, Canyoncito, the "little canyon," shows glacial polish on the rocks to one side, but none in the gorge itself, which discloses stream erosion since the retreat of the last glacier. *Willow Park,* a lovely little meadow on the left, once the bed of a small glacial lake, is a good place to see elk. Soon you leave the forest behind and enter the alpine zone, where snowbanks linger most of the year. Above lies the tundra, with plants similar to those growing above the Arctic Circle. Photograph the stone cabin at the right, and you may get a scene resembling the Swiss Alps, though "Timberline Camp" actually is used to house road crews that clear the big drift in spring.

Fall River Pass is the turn-around point of this trip. You can stop at the Alpine Visitor Center to absorb displays on alpine tundra and photograph the building and the canyon below. On the way back to Estes Park the road passes a series of overlooks with superlative views. The highest point on the road (12,183 feet) is indicated by a sign between Iceberg Lake and Fall River Pass. *Iceberg Lake* lies in the bottom of a glacial cirque, bordered by reddish volcanic cliffs. At Rock Cut, the glaciated mountains on the Continental Divide to the south appear to best advantage. You can take a short hike across a tundra nature trail, carpeted during July by low-growing colorful flowers. A five-minute walk along the path at *Forest Canyon* will bring you to a breathtaking view into the depths of the canyon and across the rugged walls of Hayden Gorge—this is one of the best places to photograph the effect of ancient glaciers in sculpturing the mountain landscape. The view from *Rainbow Curve* is vast and open, with the Great Plains far to the east and forested canyons or glacial meadows nearer at hand. Be sure to take pictures of the grotesquely formed timberline trees, reflecting the harsh climate at this altitude. *Many Parks Curve* is a good place to photograph chipmunk, Say's ground squirrel, and an attractive bird called the Clark's nutcracker at close range. To the north are excellent vistas of Fall River Valley, with the peaks of the Mummy Range towering beyond. *Hidden Valley* is the center of winter skiing, skating, and other sports. In summer you can get photos of spirelike fir and spruce, typical of the subalpine zone forest, and of beaver dams in the willow bottom.

Outstanding scenic resources also lie on the western slope of the park. Continuing from Fall River Pass, Trail Ridge Road reaches *Specimen Mountain View,* above the Cache la Poudre River. At *Milner Pass,* you cross the Continental Divide, the backbone of North America, where you can photograph the sign explaining how water flows from here to both oceans. Powerful and agile bighorn sheep, which symbolize the rugged quality of this national park, are often seen in this vicinity. Approach too closely and you may frighten them out of sight—not only for yourself but for a thousand other visitors. This is good country for elk, too. With good fortune, in September, you may capture a picture of one on a hilltop with his handsome rack outlined against a blue sky. On the way down to Grand Lake and Shadow Mountain, you may also photograph beaver, golden eagle, and hawks, depending on how lucky you are and how carefully you look. The best chances for seeing beaver are in early morning or late afternoon. Marmots are easy to spot in their rockpile homes. A good picture to use in opening or closing your coverage of Rocky Mountain National Park would be one of the distinctive blue Colorado columbine, Colorado's state flower, which is found in all climate zones, from the lowest elevations to thirteen thousand feet.

Forests, mountains, waterfalls, and wild flowers are abundant in Rocky Mountain National Park, which has few equals for sheer scenic beauty. You can drive through the park or explore it along more than three hundred miles of hiking trails.

Sequoia and Kings Canyon National Parks
Three Rivers, California 93271

These twin national parks, which are administered as a single unit, have much in common, but each has its distinctive treasures of the Sierra Nevadas. The mountains find their culmination in the summit of Mount Whitney, highest point in the country outside of Alaska. The giant sequoias reach their greatest size and largest numbers in more than thirty groves. Granite domes tower above beautiful lakes and canyons gouged deep into the earth's crust.

Sequoia was established in 1890 to preserve the Big Trees, which were then undergoing intensive logging destruction wherever they existed. Kings Canyon National Park came into being in 1940 because of its U-shaped glacial canyons—called "yosemites"—chiefly the South Fork Canyon of the Kings River, the Tehipite Canyon, and a great unspoiled wilderness in the high country. Together the two parks share one thousand miles of trail in the back country, including the famous John Muir Trail, which offers hiking opportunities along the scenic crest of the Sierras, the longest and highest mountain range in the country south of Alaska.

The parks are large in size, covering a combined total of 847,194 acres. In planning your photo schedule, consider your chances to record five distinct regions of vegetation: foothill brush or chaparral, at about fourteen hundred feet; foothill oak woodland; pine and fir forest of the middle slopes; timberline forests of stunted trees reaching up to near the mountaintops; and alpine region of moss, grass, and brief summer flowers at the edge of the snows.

Picture-Taking Stops

Turnouts and overlooks along the main roads offer many viewpoints from which to photograph spectacular scenery. If you enter Sequoia Park from the south entrance, through the town of Three Rivers, the picturesque Indian-head sign at the park gateway will make a good opening title for your picture sequence, particularly with Moro Rock, one of the great monoliths of the Sierras, in the background. You can stop at Ash Mountain park headquarters for information and guidance.

From Ash Mountain, the lowest point in Sequoia, the road, named the Generals Highway, winds upward through foothill chaparral. In early spring, blue lupine and yellow bush poppies bloom profusely. In May and June, yuccas, a member of the lily family, send up their flowers along ten- to fifteen-foot-high spikes. The booklet "Wildflowers of the Sierra," on sale at the park visitor centers, will be helpful in identification. A stop at *Arch Rock* will enable you to photograph a car going through this unusual tunnel-like formation. *Amphitheater Point* provides vistas of the highway curving up the mountain, of Hanging Rock, massive Moro Rock, and the Sierra Crest behind it. The odds are that you will see a deer or two.

Abruptly the road reaches the uplands of *Giant Forest,* the heart of Sequoia National Park, one of the greatest concentrations of forest grandeur on earth. In photographing sequoias, you'll capture the warm reddish color of the bark best in early morning and late afternoon; the light at this time of day also emphasizes the texture of the bark. The sequoias are the major attraction, but the alert photographer will observe white fir, sugar pine, chinquapin, and other interesting plants of this life community. The sugar pine is tallest of all the pines, with the largest cone, sometimes twenty inches or more in length. This area of the park, at elevations of fifty-five hundred to seven thousand feet, is beautiful to photograph in autumn, with changing colors of dogwood, hazelnut, and ferns.

Footpaths and easy drives lead to the highlights of Giant Forest in Sequoia. On the Moro Rock-Crescent Meadows Drive, the *Auto Log*, a long-dead sequoia, has been arranged so you can drive your car on it—a prominent picture point. The walk to the top of *Moro Rock* is rewarded with vistas of the Great Western Divide, the Kaweah Peaks, and San Joaquin Valley, particularly impressive with late-afternoon alpenglow. Visitors can help protect the setting by discarding used film containers in the trash receptacle at the base of the rock. After passing the *Parker Group*, an outstanding grove of Big Trees, you'll drive through the *Tunnel Log*, hollowed out of a dead sequoia. *Crescent Meadow*, surrounded by Big Trees, is a beauty spot in spring, with a carpet of wildflowers, and again in fall, when aspen trees lend their golden touch. An easy trail leads to *Tharp's Log*, the headquarters of Hale Tharp, the pioneer white man of Giant Forest, who built his cabin in a fallen sequoia log. A variety of trails start from Crescent Meadow, including one to *Eagle View Point*, one of many panoramas on the High Sierra Trail route to Bearpaw Meadow camp, where you can stay overnight at the base of the Great Western Divide.

Standing guard at the entrance to the finest part of the Giant Forest is the *General Sherman Tree*, the thirty-five-hundred-year-old giant of giants, standing 272 feet tall, with enough lumber to build forty five-room houses. The tree is a joy to photograph, being in a relatively open and unobstructed area. You can get photographs showing the whole tree from the parking area. Then move in closer for pictures of the sign detailing statistics of the tree, a member of your party looking up from the low wooden fence to indicate scale and size, and close-ups of the deeply furrowed bark. From General Sherman the self-guiding Congress Trail has many photo possibilities. Chief Sequoyah Tree, a venerable giant, gnarled and twisted, reflects the storms of ages, and honors a Cherokee leader. The *Burned Chamber*, deeply scarred by fire, demonstrates the self-healing quality of the Big Trees, part of the key to their long lives. The *President Tree* is a worthy subject not only for its size but also for its symmetry of form. A sign before the *Founders' Group* commemorates the unselfish devotion of Californians who contributed to establishment of the national park. The handsomely shaped *McKinley Tree* is the tallest in Giant Forest, while the *Telescope Tree*, near the end of the trail, is another striking example of a living sequoia with a large part of its heartwood burned out.

From Giant Forest, the Generals Highway continues past the Lodgepole Visitor Center and campground, through *Lost Grove*, which contains large and outstanding sequoias, and enters Kings Canyon National Park. The center of interest in this section of the park, Grant Grove, takes its name from the *General Grant Tree*, which is second in size to the General Sherman. Other giants in this vicinity are the General Lee Tree and the Hart Tree, fourth largest known sequoia, in Redwood Mountain Grove. The *Fallen Monarch*, a prostrate giant hollowed by fire, makes an unusual picture; so does the *Centennial Stump*, the stump of the tree cut to furnish an exhibit for the Philadelphia World's Fair of 1876. A few minutes' drive leads to *Big Stump Basin*, filled with fire-blackened reminders of early logging abuses. Another short drive and walks lead to *Panoramic Point* and *Rocking Rock*, with exceptional vistas of the Great Western Divide and Monarch Divide.

More spectacular scenery lies ahead on the drive along the South Fork of the Kings River. From an overlook you can photograph the brawling waters of the South and Middle forks where they form their junction. The road is cut into the cliffside, the river hundreds of feet below, with one breathtaking canyon view following another. Then the road dips alongside the stream; in early summer you can take pictures of the foamy white cascade, which often splashes passing cars. Beyond the lodging and food center at Cedar Grove, the road ends—appropriately at *Roads End*—where the first views unfold of mighty South Fork Canyon, which many consider as superb a scenic feature of the Sierra Nevadas as Yosemite Valley. If you walk to *Zumwalt Meadow*, three-quarters of a mile beyond, you can stand where the whole canyon opens out in a series of vistas. But this is only the beginning: the back country is accessible over about a thousand miles of trail. Many families make an annual adventure of backpacking, travel with burro or horses (which are easily rented in the park). Evolution Basin, Copper Creek, Paradise Valley, Tehipite Valley, and Simpson Meadow are a few of the places where photo-visitors find the unspoiled natural scene. From Roads End, hikers can climb to Mount Bago, then follow the John Muir Trail along the west side of the range crest, enjoying the high lakes and ultimately reaching the base of craggy Mount Whitney.

Sequoia National Park was established to preserve the giant Sequoia trees for which the park is named. It encompasses more than thirty groves of these monstrous trees, as well as granite domes towering above beautiful lakes and canyons.

Shenandoah National Park
Luray, Virginia 22835

In the heart of the Blue Ridge Mountains, Shenandoah spreads its gentle slopes and cool, shady coves and splashes them with waterfalls. Here you can see the first Appalachian peaks south of the Adirondacks that rise above four thousand feet. Shenandoah is a long, slender park, covering 212,304 acres. It is especially noted for the Skyline Drive, which winds along the highland crest for 105 miles, and for the hiker's route, the Appalachian Trail—both should be explored.

A soft mist sometimes swirls through the mountains. Occasionally you may find yourself driving above the clouds. The alert photographer capitalizes on these conditions to interpret the untamed beauty of the Blue Ridge. The park is open all year (except during brief periods following severe icing or snow-storms) and wears different faces with the changing seasons. Those who choose early spring will enjoy the blossoming of dogwood, redbud, and a host of wildflowers, followed in May by masses of pink azalea and white pendant blossoms of black locust. In June, pink and white mountain laurel announce the beginning of summer. Autumn brings a blaze of color that matches New England's best. Winter in the highlands offers evergreens standing out boldly against the snowy mountain background and icicles cascading over the cliffs.

The Blue Ridge represents an important geological story, with a chance to photograph granitic rocks which expose more than a billion years of earth forces. The naturalist program at visitor centers, campfires, and guided walks will help you identify and understand the formations.

Picture-Taking Stops

Seventy-five overlooks flare outward from the Skyline Drive. To the west, Shenandoah Valley stretches like a hazy checkerboard around Massanutten Mountain to the Allegheny Mountains beyond. In this direction you'll get many good sunset shots from the northern and central districts of the park. To the east, the gentle rolling Piedmont hills, tapering off to the coastal plains, are remnants of vast mountain ranges long since eroded away.

Entering from the north, the *Shenandoah Valley Overlook* furnishes the first view of the valley, nine hundred feet below, and the gateway town of Front Royal. At Dickey Ridge Visitor Center a ranger-naturalist might direct you to the *Snead Fire Road,* one of many locked roads through the park used only for administration and fire protection. A pleasant short walk leads to an apple orchard left by former inhabitants who farmed the uplands before the park was established. The panoramic view of Shenandoah Valley from *Signal Knob Overlook* makes an excellent sunset shot, particularly if you capture the sunset's reflection in the winding Shenandoah River. Signal Knob—the high point at the end of the second ridge—was used by both armies as a signal post during the Civil War. From *Hogwallow Flats Overlook,* if the day is clear, you'll be able to see the eleven bends in the Shenandoah River and four different mountain ranges, from the Blue Ridge to the Alleghenies.

Passing the Thornton Gap Interchange (which provides access to nearby Luray), *Marys Rock Tunnel*, bored through seven hundred feet of mountain, exposes granodiorite, an ancient basement or core rock formed deep below the earth's surface. At Shaver Hollow parking area a trail leads to *Nicholson Hollow*, lined with old mountain homesteads—log structures, fences, and weathered gravestones—traces of a vanished culture. *Corbin Cabin* is especially interesting since it has been restored and put to use as an overnight quarters for campers, available on reservation. *Stony Man Overlook* furnishes spacious views of Page Valley. An easy trail leads to the summit of *Stony Man Mountain*, one of the most prominent of Shenandoah's peaks. Viewed from the north, its profile resembles that of a man. Of geologic interest is the columnar jointing of Precambrian outcrops, typical of the Blue Ridge. You can also see these at Hawksbill, Franklin Cliffs, and Crescent Rock. Shoot a picture of one or two members of your party perched on Stony Man Cliffs with the valley stretching out three thousand feet below.

An easy and rewarding naturalist-led hike on the *Limberlost Trail* begins at the Old Rag Fire Road and leads through a grove of virgin hemlocks four and five centuries old, growing in company with red spruce, Canada yew, and other plants normally found far to the north. In walking through the virgin forests, you'll see many trees of contorted shapes that represent the drama of continuing life: one may have been struck by lightning, another damaged by ice. But the forest is constantly and patiently restoring itself with many life forms, as you can tell by observing shelf fungus feeding on some overmature trees, mushrooms on the forest floor, and the wide variety of shrubs, vines, and herbs. Continuing past the Limberlost, the trail leads to the upper reaches of *Whiteoak Canyon*, where a beautiful mountain stream drops fifteen hundred feet in less than a mile, with six major waterfalls, deep pools, and bubbling cascades.

At Hawksbill Gap parking area you can join the guided hike (during summer) on a section of the Appalachian Trail to the crest of *Hawksbill Mountain*, the highest point in the park (4,049 feet). The trail cuts across steep talus slopes of lava-formed greenstone, a prominent feature of the park, really greenish-blue in color; include a person in your picture to indicate the scale of the outcrops. The nearby trail shelter, built of native stone and oak, is the celebrated *Byrd's Nest No. 2*, one of four such camping shelters given to the park by the late Senator Harry F. Byrd, a champion of the park. His favorite route led up the east side of the park to the rocky crest of Old Rag Mountain.

Big Meadows is the center of much interest and activity. The *Harry F. Byrd Visitor Center* contains exhibits and dioramas on early mountain life and culture. The easy trail to *Dark Hollow Falls* leads to the most popular waterfalls in the park, set in a wooded ravine—it is best photographed in morning light. The road through Big Meadows across from the Byrd Center affords an excellent chance for photographing wildlife, particularly in the evening. Under park protection, the graceful whitetail deer have lost their fear of man. Some well-intentioned visitors feed the deer, serving only to destroy the animals' self-reliance and often to make them ill. Skunks, foxes, and bobcats are abroad chiefly after dark. If you walk down the Rapidan Fire Road, the trail along the stream leads to *Camp Hoover*, originally built by President Herbert Hoover as a fishing retreat. The hemlock-shaded buildings are still in limited use by the National Park Service, but visitors are welcome in the area and may take outside pictures. If you are at Big Meadows during the summer and ask directions, you will be treated to the sight of chestnut trees in bloom.

These great trees once covered the Blue Ridge but are now doomed by blight; still a few grow large enough to bear flowers.

Continuing south on the Skyline Drive, park naturalists lead hikes during the summer from the Bear Fence Mountain parking area over an attractive section of the Appalachian Trail to *Bear Fence Mountain* with a scramble over the rocks—potential for a lively movie sequence, capped with good views of the valley from the top. Another hike leads from Smith Roach Gap to *Hightop Mountain,* with an excellent view of the surrounding country. *Loft Mountain Campground* is equipped with a new modern amphitheater; you may want to take close-up flash pictures at the evening campfires. At *Sawmill Run Overlook,* the Appalachian Trail crosses the Skyline Drive. You can follow the hikers on their route by walking half a mile to Sawmill Run Shelter. At *Rockfish Gap* take pictures of the signs that show where Shenandoah National Park joins the Blue Ridge Parkway, which continues the high road through Virginia and North Carolina to link with the Great Smoky Mountains National Park.

Shenandoah National Park is noted for its Skyline Drive, which winds along the highland crest for more than one hundred miles, and for the Appalachian Trail, which is a popular hiking route. You can see wild flowers in the spring and summer, and a blaze of colorful foliage in the fall.

Virgin Islands National Park
St. John, Virgin Islands 00830

White-sand beaches and coral gardens in the blue-green Caribbean waters fringe the smallest island in the Virgin Islands of the United States. Nearly two-thirds of this island—St. John—have been set aside as a national park, a total of 15,150 acres, complete with tropical forest, unusual plant life, old Danish ruins, and quiet coves.

Seascapes, tropical sunsets, and lush foliage will appeal to all photo-visitors. But the most unusual photographic subjects in the Virgin Islands are found underwater. The delicately balanced life community below the surface is challenging and rewarding to record, with its spectacle of schools of brilliant fish swimming through castles of coral and swaying plants. If you can swim well and have fins and snorkel, you can shoot underwater pictures with almost any camera—but you must first install it in a special water-tight camera housing (many types of which are now available). The waters around St. John are best for underwater photography from July through November; during other months heavy sea swells tend to keep the water cloudy several days each week. Even under ideal conditions, however, underwater photography *is* different. Due to refraction, subjects look closer than they actually are. Exposure of pictures depends on many things—angle of the sun, clarity of the water, depth, color of the bottom, and nearness of the subject. An automatic camera takes variables into consideration and will give you good exposure; with a camera that has a maximum lens opening of approximately $f/8$ or $f/11$, you can plan on taking pictures without flash on a sunny day to depths of approximately fifteen to twenty feet with an ASA 64 film. It's best to prepare carefully in all respects. Reading "The Underwater Guide to Marine Life," by Ray and Ciampi, will help; it has a chapter on underwater photography and is a good guide to the area. You may also want to buy a copy of the KODAK Book "The Fifth Here's How" (AE-87), sold by Kodak dealers. It contains a thorough article on underwater photography. Park service personnel are always willing to assist visitors with suggestions on underwater picture-taking.

Picture-Taking Stops

We've outlined a tour route starting from the Visitor Center at *Cruz Bay,* the port village, dating from Danish days. You can make the trip on the daily jeep tour booked through a travel agency, by hiring a jeep taxi with driver, or by renting a jeep and driving yourself. Note that vehicles drive on the left and that roads are narrow, winding, sometimes rocky, with little or no shoulders. The regular overlooks noted below present the best and safest stopping places, but proceed with caution anyway.

Cruz Bay offers a number of picture opportunities, including people, native houses, an old ruin, boats at the harbor, and the Visitor Center itself. Leaving the village, the route follows Centerline Road into the cool hills. Numerous colorful fruit trees, plants, and flowers line the road, serving both as close-up subjects and to help frame vistas.

The first turnout, *Kong Vey*, affords a sweeping view of the Atlantic Ocean and some of the British Virgin Islands. This is followed by a spectacular overlook of *Reef Bay Valley*, with steep hillsides that once grew sugarcane, with the ruins of the eighteenth-century Reef Bay Plantation and a splendid view of the Caribbean beyond. Rounding a sharp curve brings one over the quiet village of Coral Bay, the site of the first Danish settlement, with a breathtaking spread of the British Virgin Islands in the brilliant, calm blue sea.

At King Hill Road the route turns left and descends to the *Annaberg Sugar Mill Ruin* on the North Shore. By means of the self-guiding trail, you can photograph a phase of Danish colonial history and get interesting pictures of architectural and construction details. From Annaberg the photo tour proceeds to *Maho Bay*, a sheltered cove on the Atlantic side. Reaching the far end of the bay, one ascends along the hillside, where it is possible to view and photograph both Maho Bay and Francis Bay, the larger body to the north. A short distance beyond, *Cinnamon Bay* comes into view, and then the spectacular vista of *Trunk Bay Beach*, a cove where the rendezvous of shore and sea seems to sum up the beauty of the Caribbean. Trunk Bay is the setting of the *Underwater Snorkeling Trail*, a fascinating adaptation of National Park Service methods to interpret the natural scene. The trail reaches a depth of ten feet. With underwater camera equipment, you can take pictures of the labels etched on submerged glass plates. Other good possibilities for snorkeling are on conducted trips at Cinnamon Bay Beach and Hawksnest Beach.

Continuing on the North Shore Road, you can make good pictures at *Hawksnest Bay* and *Caneel Bay Plantation*, and then photograph the outstanding view overlooking Cruz Bay.

White sand beaches, coral gardens, blue-green Caribbean waters, tropical forests, quiet coves, and old Danish ruins make up a wonderland called Virgin Islands National Park. You can take a self-guided tour through the park to photograph a phase of Danish colonial history.

Wind Cave National Park
Hot Springs, South Dakota 57747

A portion of the original prairie grassland that once flanked the Black Hills still endures within the bounds of this national park. And with it is one of the finest displays anywhere of wildlife characteristic of the Great Plains before white men came—herds of bison, pronghorn, elk, and many smaller forms, including black-tailed prairie dogs in one of their last strongholds.

The geological features within the 28,059-acre park are outstanding too, forming a significant chapter in the history of the "Black Hills uplift." Below the surface, after the final upheaval of the land from beneath the inland sea, water forces penetrated cracks in the limestone and ultimately carved passages and rooms of what is now called Wind Cave. It derives its name from strong currents of air that sometimes blow alternately in and out. These are believed to be caused by changes in atmospheric pressure on the outside.

The park features a fine guided program to keep a photographer on the go from six A.M. to ten P.M. recording the diverse phases of the "vanishing" prairie in the western Great Plains.

Picture-Taking Stops

At six o'clock each summer morning, except Sunday, naturalists conduct a leisurely bird-watching excursion into *Wind Cave Canyon*, where you can count on seeing a number of the 140 species of birds found in the park. Among these are several of the majestic birds of prey. With patience, a portfolio of pictures in Wind Cave could include the red-tailed hawk; ferruginous hawk, which is often mistaken for an eagle because of its size; golden eagle, recognized in flight by its immense size and long, blunt-ended wings; bald eagle, easy to identify with its massive white head and tail; marsh hawk, showing its white rump patch while flying low over the ground; prairie falcon, which often feeds on insects over prairie-dog towns; and brightly colored sparrow hawk, frequently seen perching on road posts.

At seven o'clock each summer morning, except Sunday, and again in the evening at six-thirty, wildlife caravans are conducted on the park road network. For an opportunity to view and photograph unrestrained wildlife in its natural habitat, these activities in Wind Cave are unsurpassed. The bison, largest North American mammal, is the most picturesque animal in the park, and herds often show up close to the roads. This shaggy giant is unpredictable and should never be taken for granted; *it can wheel and charge in a split second.* By all means, take pictures from your parked car. In beauty of form and grace of movement, few animals can equal the pronghorn on the open plains. Its contrastingly marked body of brown and creamy white posed against a clear blue western sky makes it an outstanding subject for wildlife photographers. "Towns" of prairie dogs, which once covered thousands of square miles, are scattered throughout the park. Two of the largest are on the main park road, with their community life. You'll have more luck observing from the road than if you try to walk among the burrows; by so doing you simply chase them underground. Chances of seeing elk are good in certain parts of the park. Herds can often be seen migrating through the southern ends in the vicinity of the Bison Flat prairie-dog town; the big flat off NPS 5 in the northern end is another favorite haunt. Many other mammals are often seen, including mule deer, coyote, badger, raccoon (primarily at night), bobcat, marmot, and squirrel. Whether or not you join a wildlife caravan, remember that the best hours to observe birds and mammals are early morning and late evening. If you have the opportunity to photograph birds and mammals by back-lighting, you'll find that light playing through the tips of feathers and fur produces a "rim" effect, which adds a three-dimensional quality and separates the subject from the background.

Cave tours are conducted throughout the day. A special Photographic Tour starts at seven-thirty A.M., designed so you can carry tripod, flash, and other equipment not allowed on regular tours and without being restricted by a timetable. This is not the largest cave in the world, but it's a fun cave to photograph. A park naturalist leads the group to interesting subjects, such as the intricate boxwork formations in the Post Office Room and Elks Room, frostwork in the Garden of Eden and Fairgrounds, and more delicate frostwork near the Pearly Gates.

Varying hikes are conducted at all hours of the day, affording a chance to behold the beauty of a sea of wild grass rippling in the wind and to interpret on film the individual blades of blue grama, western wheatgrass, little bluestem, and threadleaf sedge which make this park a unique mixture of the true prairie and the short-grass plains. A sprinkling of wildflowers lends color to the scene in spring and summer. The park is a meeting place of eastern and western flora, where you will find the pale blue pasqueflower (South Dakota's state flower), dark-throat shooting star, Rocky Mountain iris, prairie coneflower, and bluebell mixed with yucca, cactus, and cottonwood. The "Natural History Story of Wind Cave," sold at the Visitors Center, will help you identify these when you see and photograph them.

Yellowstone National Park
Wyoming 83020

The nation's largest and oldest national park is filled with attractions both widespread and diverse. The key quality is its naturalness—the park was established in 1872 when the West was still young, and most of the immense domain is still unaltered and unspoiled by man, despite the endless throng of visitors. The challenge to the photographer, or any park visitor, is to capture the pristine wilderness scenery, the historic natural tableau which John Colter, Jim Bridger, and other early explorers knew.

This requires time in a park that covers 2,221,773 acres. One can't speed through Yellowstone and absorb the significance of the thousands of geysers, hot springs, and bubbling mud volcanoes; the plant life and wildlife; the canyons, lakes, and streams. These are all part of the color and beauty of the park, and whether the visitor is on his first or fifteenth trip he should allow ample time. Certain specific steps will help you make the best use of your time. Many publications can be read in advance to supplement this photo guide in preparing for the Yellowstone experience. When you arrive, many fine publications for evening reading are available at stores and visitor centers. Attend as many campfire talks as possible—plan your days to include these programs both for information and picture-taking ideas.

Although most park visitors come during the summer peak, some photographers prefer to come earlier or later. In May, June, September, and October, you might be greeted by a light snow, but make the most of it. It adds a new sort of beauty to the scene, and the spotty cross-lighting that precedes or follows snowfall can be quite dramatic for a few fleeting minutes. In May and June, snow still covers the mountain summits, presenting a contrast to blue skies, while the same period is marked by flowers in full bloom in the lowlands. Animals are far more in evidence in spring and fall than in summer, when they scatter over the high country. Winter is quite a new Yellowstone visitor season and a popular one. The concession-operated Motor Inn at Mammoth, near the north entrance, is open all year and is the starting point for tours in heated snowmobiles to various parts of the park. The spectacular winter panorama includes herds of bison grazing in geyser basins, where warmth keeps the snow melted and exposes the grass; elk plowing through the deep snow in search of food; a fawn with snow on its muzzle from winter grazing; Old Faithful spouting against a background of snowbank and sky, and steam rising from thermal features over bordering ice formations.

Use a fast shutter speed to photograph the geysers. It's best to photograph hot pools on warm days, when steam doesn't obscure the subjects. Clean your camera lens with a soft, lintless cloth after leaving each area, since silica residues stick to the surface once they dry. Early morning and late afternoon are the best time to photograph thermal attractions. Side-lighting and back-lighting add dimension and pictorial quality.

Early morning and late afternoon are also the best hours to find wildlife at various points along their routes of travel. Black bear can be seen almost anywhere along park roads during the summer season, but always photograph them from inside your automobile or at a very safe distance.

If you need film, or questions answered, Haynes Photo Shops throughout the park are extremely well equipped.

Picture-Taking Stops

The best-known features are on the 145-mile Grand Loop Road, with a series of activity centers on the way. Use these as the gateways to photographing the Yellowstone wilderness by foot, horseback, or boat, all of which can easily be done—the park has more than a thousand miles of well-marked trail—and will give a deep feeling of the country.

Starting at the south entrance (a few miles north of Grand Teton National Park), you can photograph the entrance sign announcing your arrival and start on the road north along the Lewis River. You'll find many turnouts at

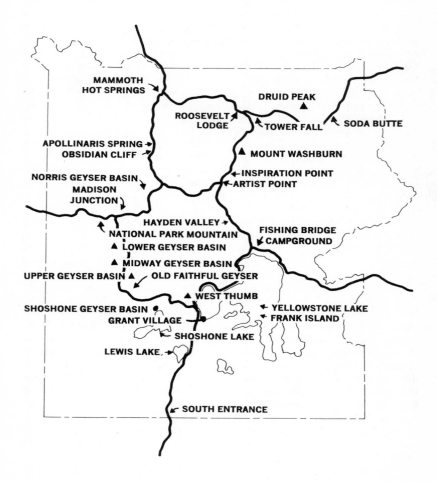

scenic vistas and explanatory signs to use as titles in your pictures. Lewis Lake is the start of the trail through splendid scenic country to *Shoshone Lake,* one of the major lakes of the park, which cannot be reached by car. It is also accessible by canoe, but not by motorboat. The reward for one's effort is to camp in the wilderness and explore the *Shoshone Geyser Basin.* Continuing by road leads one to *West Thumb* on the shore of *Yellowstone Lake,* one of the most inspiring bodies of water in the world, with its sparkling waters and fringe of forest and snowy mountains. A guided two-hour walk each day leads to a scenic overlook above the lake. Walks are also conducted several times a day through Thumb Geyser Basin, noted for Abyss and Black pools, two of the largest hot springs in the park, and the Fishing Cone, a seething hot spring in the cold water of the lake. How many such features can you photograph? There are ten thousand throughout the park, mostly in rather well-defined basins. You would do well to learn the various kinds—geysers (fountain type and cone type), hot springs, mud pots, mud volcanoes, mud geysers, and fumaroles—and then choose representations of each for a picture portfolio of the park.

Driving clockwise, the Grand Loop follows the shoreline with several excellent viewpoints and a side road leading to the Natural Bridge, a forty-foot-high stone arch. The *Lake Area* and nearby *Fishing Bridge* are major centers of varied activity. One of the best things you can do here is to get on the great lake itself. The simplest way is aboard the forty-passenger excursion boat for an hour-long cruise; with good luck you may see ducks, geese, and pelicans, and possibly moose browsing along the shoreline. You can rent a motorboat for fishing and sightseeing on your own. One of the finest trips would take you to *Frank Island* to observe osprey, or fish hawks, in their wilderness treetop nesting places. The ultimate experience would be to hire a rowboat and be hauled by boat taxi to Plover Point, gateway to the famous south arms, where motors are prohibited, for wilderness camping in a world of pelicans, cormorants, and gulls. For another perspective from the Lake Area, join the half-day Elephant Back Hike to gain a lofty view of the irregular shoreline.

Hayden Valley, a large grassland-sagebrush area on the Grand Loop north of the lake, is the summer home of many elk. There is a good chance of spotting grizzly bears in this region too. Should you have this good fortune, exercise respect and extreme caution. Here one learns to appreciate the vastness of Yellowstone as the essential roaming room which the grizzly, elk, bighorn sheep, and bison require to live, breed, and die in natural ways. *Canyon Village* is another major center, providing access to the vividly colored *Grand Canyon* of the Yellowstone River, a breathtaking spectacle from Artist, Inspiration, Grandview, Lookout, or any other point along its twenty-four-mile course. The precipitous walls glow with reds, ochers, and yellows. The view from Artist Point, in particular, of the majestic Lower Falls of the Yellowstone River has been favored by artists and photographers since the first explorers came this way. A choice all-day hike from Canyon Village leads through forest and flowering meadows to the snowy summit of Mount Washburn, capped by a breathtaking view from the lookout tower. Such lookout stations in parks and forests are interesting places for the photographer, because they are invariably situated at locations with sweeping panoramas. If you prefer not to hike, you can reach the summit on a sightseeing bus from the base, but the adventure is worth it one way or the other.

In the *Tower Junction* area, there is a pleasant detour on the leisurely old

Tower Fall Road. Then follow the footpath to see *Tower Fall* plunging 132 feet from a pinnacle brink of sharp rock. *Roosevelt Lodge,* Yellowstone's dude ranch, affords a chance for horseback riding for an hour, a half day, or all day. The horses are "broke gentle," so you'll be able to take pictures without dismounting as long as your mount is standing still—stick plenty of film in your pockets and carry your camera around your neck. Another possibility here is the stagecoach ride to Pleasant Valley, aboard a sturdy Concord of the kind used for sightseeing in the pre-gasoline age. There is also an all-day hike to *Specimen Ridge Fossil Forest,* part of the largest known area of petrified trees in the world; unlike the trees in the Petrified Forest in Arizona, which are strewn and scattered, the petrified pines, walnuts, chestnuts, and others of Yellowstone are mostly still standing upright. Lamar Valley, between Tower Junction and the northeast entrance, is a good region for antelope, coyote, and other wildlife.

Near the north entrance, Mammoth Hot Springs is the site of park headquarters and center of huge steaming travertine terraces and pools of delicate shapes colored by algae, which you can photograph at close range from wooden walks. The guided walk starts at the Liberty Cap, a huge rock created by an ancient hot spring that went dry; it makes a fine picture when you include people to indicate the size of the rock. Turning south, the Grand Loop passes *Obsidian Cliffs,* composed of a type of black volcanic glass, then comes to the spectacular *Norris Geyser Basin.* In early morning, steam condenses in the cold air to form drifting white plumes over the hot springs and geysers, creating an interesting effect in photographs. *Gibbon Falls,* plunging eighty-four feet along the Gibbon, is easy to reach from a parking area on the way to *Madison Junction,* which links the Grand Loop with the west entrance. A marker by the roadside, where the Firehole and Gibbon rivers meet under the shadow of National Park Mountain, marks the site of the historic campfire where members of the Washburn-Langford-Doane Expedition of 1870 conceived the revolutionary idea of setting this great area aside as "a public park or pleasuring ground for the benefit and enjoyment of the people." A photo taken here could be the opening or closing of your Yellowstone sequence, if not of your entire national-parks picture story.

The Firehole River, paralleling the road, snakes through half a dozen steaming geyser basins in approaching the culmination of Yellowstone's thermal wonders. First comes the *Lower Geyser Basin,* the largest thermal area in the park, which includes the colorful Fountain Paint Pot, Red Spouter, Gentian Pool, and Firehole Pool. From the side of Roaring Mountain, steam rises from hundreds of vents. Next comes the Midway Geyser Basin, with Grand Prismatic Spring, the largest spring in the park, and then *Upper Geyser Basin,* covering about two square miles, with beautiful and unusual-shaped hot-water displays bearing such fitting names as Grotto Geyser, Castle Geyser, Coral Geyser, and Mustard Springs. Finally the road arrives at *Old Faithful,* the majestic symbol of Yellowstone. It may not be the largest or most spectacular geyser, but it *is* the most regular. Its display seems most impressive in cool weather or early morning, when superheated water meets cold air and condenses into billowing clouds of steam. Twilight is another interesting time, particularly if you're shooting in color. From Observation Point, high above the geyser, the view embraces a broad panorama, including Old Faithful Inn, a museum piece of another day, and the forested Madison Plateau. From here it is a short drive to complete the Grand Loop at West Thumb, passing Shoshone Point and crossing the Continental Divide.

Yosemite National Park
California 95389

The Sierra Nevadas, the "Range of Light," which constitute one of the most inspiring and hospitable assemblages of mountains in the world, reach their climax within the boundaries of this national park. Its beauties have been known, loved, and recorded for a long time.

Indians chose it as a favored dwelling place for centuries. The first tourist party came in 1855, in the days when photography was still young, but a San Francisco publisher brought along an artist and then published his sketches of the newly found wonderland. Yosemite was not the first national park, but as early as 1864—eight years before the establishment of Yellowstone—Congress voted to grant Yosemite Valley and the Mariposa Big Tree Grove to the state of California in order to protect them from private exploitation and to preserve them for public use.

Yosemite is a picture-taker's delight, where photographers can prowl about for hours and days and in all seasons. The most outstanding features are the lofty *granite domes and spires* rising above glacial-carved canyons; *waterfalls* of unusual height and beauty; groves of *giant sequoias* that humble the viewer with their size, age, and stately proportions; and the *high country* of the Sierras, with its picturesque peaks, lakes, and meadows. Because of the wide range in elevation, from the warm foothills to the Arctic-Alpine zone above timberline, there are over thirteen hundred species of flowering plants and many species of trees.

Many of the unusual rock formations are as striking in black and white as in color. Ansel Adams, famous for his photographic interpretations of natural scenes, has been demonstrating this for years. Adams has trained many persons in photography and appreciation of nature, simultaneously, and continues to conduct his Yosemite Photography Workshop each summer. You will also derive much inspiration from the book "Gentle Wilderness—The Sierra Nevada," published by the Sierra Club, with magnificent photographs by Richard Kauffman and matching text by John Muir, the master of these mountains.

For the photographer, seasons in Yosemite are what he makes of them. Spring to many is ideal, when the waterfalls leap in the flood of melting snows and wildflowers spread carpets of color across the lower meadows. (When you get close to the falls, protect your camera from the water spray.) Summer is time to head for the spacious subalpine meadows and glistening lakes of the high country. Autumn flashes brilliantly, but the park tempo is unhurried, allowing plenty of time for taking pictures of colorful oaks, maples, dogwoods, and aspens. In winter Yosemite Valley and the road to Badger Pass offer excellent opportunities for photography after a storm, when the trees are laden with a mantle of snow. In late winter tiny bright-yellow flowers burst forth from the limbs of giant sequoias in a delicate golden spray that invites photographers to take close-up pictures.

The park covers 760,951 acres and lies about one hundred and fifty miles southeast of San Francisco. Two of the four entrances are open all year—the south entrance, fifty-nine miles from Fresno, and Arch Rock entrance, sixty-seven miles from Merced.

Picture-Taking Stops

From the south entrance, the first major point of interest is the *Mariposa Grove,* the largest of three sequoia stands in the park. The most famous and most photographed of the old giants is the Wawona Tunnel Tree, which was cut in 1881 for stagecoach traffic and is wide enough for any automobile. The Grizzly Giant is the largest in Yosemite and the fifth largest giant sequoia in the world. Though estimated to be thirty-eight hundred years old, it still produces cones. Among other trees of interest are the Corridor Tree and Clothespin Tree, which have been scarred by fire through the centuries. Include people in your pictures to demonstrate scale.

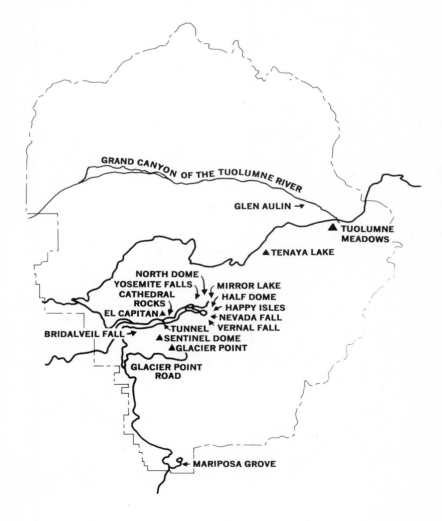

Driving on park roads is different from driving on highways. The roads are designed to provide vistas and let you step out of your car occasionally to walk under the trees or to the falls. After passing through the *Wawona Tunnel,* the panorama of Yosemite Valley unfolds from one of the finest photo vantage points in America, embracing *El Capitan,* the imposing massive granite block, larger than Gibraltar; Bridal Veil Falls, a beautiful 620-foot cataract; the Cathedral Rocks rising above the waters; and Half Dome, projecting on the distant skyline. This is a view that presents ever-changing faces at different hours of the day and in different seasons. Take overall pictures of the principal features, then photograph them from different angles as you tour Yosemite Valley.

The profound gorge, called *Yosemite Valley,* or the "Incomparable Valley," cut by the Merced River and gouged by glaciers, is walled by mountain-sized rocks, separated by side canyons with many picture-taking opportunities. The upper end of the Yosemite Valley Drive is a one-way road, which means you can stop almost anywhere, allowing plenty of room for traffic to go around you in safety.

Bridal Veil Meadows, carpeted with wildflowers, will probably be your first highlight in the valley. *Bridal Veil Falls* and their misty plumes run all year, but diminish in late summer. On sunny days in spring and early summer you'll have a good chance to shoot afternoon rainbows in the spray from the base of the falls. The twin *Cathedral Spires,* rising twenty-one hundred and nineteen hundred feet above the valley floor, dominate the south-rim skyline. On the opposite side of the valley, the *Three Brothers* rise one above the other to reach the highest point on the north rim, thirty-eight hundred feet above the floor. In photographing such formations, study the sunlight and shadows that emphasize the dimensions and texture of the rock.

At Yosemite Village, the *Visitor Center* contains outstanding exhibits and mounted large-scale photographs illustrating various features of the park. During the summer, demonstrations of Indian basketry are presented outdoors, affording a chance to photograph the oldest native art form of the Sierras. You'll find many points from which to shoot *Yosemite Falls,* one of the highest waterfalls in the world, which is at its best from April to June. By following the trail from the parking area to the base, you can get an intimate picture with telephoto lens of the great Upper Fall, which plunges 1,430 feet. To the right of the Upper Fall, *Low Arrow* rises several hundred feet as a slender shaft of granite apart from the main cliff.

You can take many pictures using the serene Merced River as a foreground. Deer are common in the valley but should not be approached too closely. The meadows of grass, fern, azaleas, dogwood, oaks, and pines have a beauty of their own—though because of various changes they are mere remnants of the wide, open meadows that inspired early visitors. Sentinel Bridge crosses the river, affording an excellent view of *Half Dome,* one of the classic Yosemite formations, which dominates the upper end of the valley. From the vicinity of the LeConte Memorial, a picturesque stone building, where the Sierra Club maintains summer mountaineering headquarters, there are fine views of the *Royal Arches* and *Washington Column,* which juts above the valley floor like a tall skyscraper three times higher than the Washington Monument; rising above both is *North Dome.* Nearing the base of Half Dome, the Merced River branches into several channels, forming the *Happy Isles,* where the visitor center is devoted to wilderness recreation with displays of back-packing gear. Trails lead from here in many directions, including the aptly named Mist Trail to *Vernal Fall* and *Nevada Fall*, which bring the river tumbling into the valley.

At the end of the valley loop road lies *Mirror Lake;* reflections are nearest perfect in early morning and late afternoon. By walking the path along the lakeshore, you can photograph *Clouds Rest*, the highest mountain visible from Yosemite Valley; and across the canyon *Mount Watkins* is often reflected in the lake.

The Glacier Point Road leads up to outstanding panoramic vistas of the High Sierras. It passes through a red-fir forest, then crosses Bridal Veil Creek, the source of water for Bridal Veil Falls. A side road and short path lead to the summit of *Sentinel Dome*, which affords not only an excellent view of the valley but also a chance for close-ups of exfoliation shells, the weathering process characteristic of Yosemite. The stunted and contorted Jeffrey pine at this site is one of the most photographed trees in the world. *Washburn Point* is another good photographic stop, facing Half Dome and the sweeping Sierras. *Glacier Point Lookout*, the climax of the drive, is a classic and inspiring viewpoint of the park, embracing the high country, the great domes standing out in bold relief, Yosemite Falls, Tenaya Canyon, Nevada Falls and Vernal Falls plummeting down the Little Yosemite, and the narrow valley far below. You can take outstanding pictures here with the alpenglow at sunset. From here you can hike down over the scenic Four Mile Trail, part of the seven-hundred-mile trail network in the park.

The Tioga Road passes through the high country of lakes, meadows, and domes, with opportunity to photograph some of the highlights of Yosemite Valley from surprising and different angles. Often the road is lined with snow even in July, which adds an interesting dimension to your pictures. Along the roadside, manzanita shrubs are especially striking subjects, with snow on the leaves and sun glinting the red bark. In autumn the road is landscaped with golden aspen. From the turnout at *Olmsted Point* a trail leads to a nearby dome for fine views down Tenaya Canyon to Half Dome and up the canyon to Tenaya Lake beneath the Sierra Crest. In this vicinity you'll see many fine patches of glacial polish, shining as bright as a mirror in early morning and afternoon. *Tenaya Lake*, one of the largest and most beautiful lakes in the park, is also surrounded by fine examples of glacial polish, for the lake basin was excavated by moving ice. *Tuolumne Meadows*, an attractive area flanked by imposing domes, is the takeoff point for hiking and riding trails of varying length in the High Sierras. The park concession conducts week-long trips afoot to permanent trail camps, enabling travelers to go light to areas of scenic beauty. A ranger-naturalist leads the way to such points as Glen Aulin, at the foot of the spectacular series of falls made by the Tuolumne River in its drop to the Grand Canyon of the Tuolumne, one of the wonders of the Sierras safeguarded in the national-park wilderness.

Zion National Park
Springdale, Utah 84767

The arid desert and canyon landscape of southern Utah blazes in color, which reaches a climax of brilliance at Zion Canyon. In this narrow, curving gorge nature has carved and painted sandstone and shale cliffs and temples. "Nothing can exceed the wonderful beauty of Zion," an early geologist recorded. "In the nobility and beauty of the sculptures there is no comparison."

Zion Canyon, the heart of the 147,035-acre park, is largely the work of the Virgin River, which has opened and laid bare the pages of geological history through endless centuries of erosive cutting, supplemented by wind, frost, and rain. Yet the brilliant colors of the cliffs are softened by the green of the cottonwoods, ash, and maples along the river and by the hanging gardens of columbine, shooting star, and cardinal flowers. The colorful "Zion moonflower" opens in the evening and wilts beneath the sun's rays in the morning.

As a rule, most peaks on the west wall make good pictures in the morning before 10:30; those on the east wall are good in the afternoon after 2:30; but many fine pictures can be taken at any time of day. Late afternoon and sunset are excellent hours, affording the dimensions of clouds, deep shadows, and cliffs in many shades of red.

The park is open all year, and each season has its own appeal. In winter, colored cliffs stand out in contrast to snow-covered terraces and slopes. Spring brings fresh flowers and new foliage. Late summer is the blooming time of asters and paintbrush. Autumn is marked with clear skies and brilliant reds and yellows creeping up the ravines.

Picture-Taking Stops

Approaching from the east, on the Zion-Mt. Carmel Highway, you can make the most effective photographs of *Checkerboard Mesa* in the morning from about one hundred yards west of the turnout and fifty yards south of the road. Have someone stand on the mountain for interest. You can photograph the pattern of cross-bedded deposits, which account for the name "Checkerboard," to tell the story of Zion's geology in pictures, later adding specimens of Navajo sandstone, Carmel limestone, and the ancient Moenkopi. Before entering the Zion Tunnel, a self-guiding trail follows rock ledges through piñon, juniper, yucca, and cacti to the *Canyon Overlook*, above the Great Arch, for a magnificent view of the canyon and the famous Zion switchbacks; photography is best in the morning. The *Great Arch of Zion* can be shown to advantage from the uppermost east-facing switchback below the tunnel in late afternoon.

After stopping at the Visitor Center, near the south entrance, the *West Temple*, Zion's highest peak, soaring 4,015 feet above the valley, and the Towers of the Virgin can be photographed from the grounds outside. Shadows are most effective shortly after noon. The *Watchman*, in the southern section of the park, is good in either the morning or the afternoon from the camp-

Through countless centuries, the Virgin River, together with wind, frost, and rain, has worked to create the towering cliffs of Zion National Park. The brilliant colors of the cliffs are softened by the cottonwoods, ash, and maples along the river, and by the hanging gardens of columbine.

ground area and makes a study in contrast if photographed at both times. To the north, the Zion Canyon Scenic Drive, a round trip of twelve miles, provides a constantly changing vista of multicolored cliffs. First are the *Mountain of the Sun* and the *Twin Brothers;* the tall trees on either side of the road provide a handy frame for a picture. Then come the *Three Patriarchs*, which are best in late morning from the upper viewpoint above the parking area; if you have a wide-angle lens, you can get them all in one picture. The *Emerald Pools Trail*, a naturalist-led walk, crosses the quiet-flowing Virgin River (which transforms into a torrent during cloudbursts in the high country) on footbridges to end at a pool formed by waterfalls. *Angels Landing,* the flattop mountain rising fifteen hundred feet above the river, can be photographed from the vicinity of the Grotto picnic area, preferably in early afternoon. A fairly strenuous 2 1/2-mile trail leads to the summit, with beautiful views of the canyon as the reward. Facing the opposite direction from the Grotto area, your camera will pick up *Red Arch Mountain*. Then comes the most striking formation of all, the *Great White Throne*, the symbol of Zion itself, a mighty twenty-four-hundred-foot monolith that shades upward from the base in deep red to pink and white. It is best photographed in the afternoon from two pull-outs just north of the Weeping Rock parking area—from the upper pullout you may want to wade across the Virgin River and shoot from high on the opposite hillside. A wide-angle lens is recommended but not necessary. The same parking area is the start of the *East Rim Trail*, a seven-mile trip following an old Indian path past beautiful narrow canyons and water-scoured rocks, with breathtaking views of Angels Landing; Great White Throne; and Cable, Cathedral, and Lady mountains. The trail is fairly difficult, but a spectacular vista awaits the hiker at Observation Point, the end of the trail.

As Zion Canyon steadily narrows, the road reaches the Temple of Sinawava, the takeoff point for the naturalist-guided *Narrows Trail* trip following the Virgin River to the Hanging Gardens of Zion, where seepage springs have created an environment for moisture-loving plants high on the canyon wall. Several routes lead into canyons and high, forested plateaus for overnight trips into the roadless wilderness. One of the best, the *Kolob Trail*, follows an excellent back-packing and horseback route with good campsites, and a side trip to the Kolob Arch, even higher than the famous Rainbow Bridge. The remote Kolob Canyons contain some of southern Utah's most outstanding scenery.